Hodder Gibson

Scottish Examination Materials

ENGLISH
Essay Skills

for
Intermediate 2, Higher
and Advanced Higher

Mary M Firth
Andrew G Ralston

Illustrations by
O. R. Davison
and M. E. Ralston

HODDER
GIBSON
PART OF HACHETTE LIVRE UK

CONTENTS

INTRODUCTION

This new edition of *Essay Skills* has been revised to accommodate changes in the current examination arrangements. The aim of this edition remains the same: to teach you the skills needed for the various types of essay required for Higher and Intermediate 2 English courses. These skills and techniques are also applicable to work in Advanced Higher and Advanced Level English.

The essay writing that you will be doing as part of these courses will fall into two broad categories.

1. *Writing critical essays on literary texts*

   You will be given a choice of writing about prose, poetry and drama texts composed by various authors. Sometimes you will be able to write about a text you have studied in school or college under the guidance of a teacher, and sometimes you will have to make the choice of text yourself. At the end of this book there is a list of recommended texts for this purpose.

2. *Writing in a particular genre*

   This is writing which you *yourself* compose. A 'genre' is a particular type or category of writing, such as prose fiction. There are always specific guidelines with reference to length or the conditions under which the writing must be done. Your teacher or tutor will be able to inform you of the rules which you must follow.

PART ONE

Writing a Critical Essay

I : *Understanding the Theory*

"Nothing is as practical as theory."
(J. Robert Oppenheimer (1904-67), American Physicist)

WHAT YOU WILL BE ASKED TO DO

You will have to write critical essays in response to a question.

- In the case of external exams, you will be set a question which you must attempt to answer in your essay. There will be a limited number of questions from which to choose. Your teacher or tutor will tell you how many essays must be written and what the time limit is.
- In the case of internal assessments, you may be given a set question, or you may be asked to choose your own topic. This will depend on the precise course you are following.

WHAT THE EXAMINER IS LOOKING FOR

The points you will be assessed on are as follows.

- Secure **understanding** of the ideas in the text.
- Accurate and detailed **analysis** of the style.
- **Evaluation** of the effectiveness of the text based firmly on textual evidence.
- **Expression**, which includes the use of appropriate critical terms, communicates your meaning clearly and develops a line of thought.

WHAT THIS SECTION DEALS WITH

The aim of this section is to take you through the entire process of writing a critical essay stage by stage:

> *reading the question*
> *planning the essay*
> *beginning the essay*
> *developing the essay*
> *ending the essay.*

The basic methods of critical essay construction are the same whether you are entering at Intermediate, Higher or Advanced level.

Stage One:
Reading the Question

The most important piece of advice that anyone can give you about writing a critical essay is simply to **answer the question**. Even if your essay is the right length, displays knowledge of the text and is written in perfect English style, it will not be acceptable if it does not focus on what the question is asking you to do.

Few people would immediately start writing their answer without reading the question — but many just read it quickly and then go ahead to write something they have prepared beforehand.

The starting point of your critical essay should *not* **be the** *text* **you have studied, but the** *question* **you are answering**. You should learn to recognise the significance of certain phrases which often appear in essay questions. Here are some of them:

> *"by close reference to the text . . ."*
>> This obviously means that you are expected to include detailed examples of points you make, referring to specific events in the story. Often close reference to the text will take the form of quotations.

> *"to what extent . . ."*
>> — as in, for example, "to what extent does the character learn important truths about himself / herself in the course of the play?" This allows you to discuss both the extent to which he / she *does* learn these truths, and the extent to which he / she *does not*. It leaves it up to you to decide whether you want to argue "yes, he does", "no, he doesn't" or "in some ways he does and in other ways he doesn't". This last approach is likely to be the best as most good literature is fairly complex and a one-sided response will probably be too simplistic.

> *"discuss the various techniques by which the writer presents . . ."*
>> The use of the word *techniques* indicates that you are expected not just to consider the content of the book, play or poem, but the story-telling *methods* used by the writer, the use of description, figures of speech, and so on. One of the most common faults in answers to this kind of question is for students to say too much about the story itself and not enough about the techniques used.

In reading the question, then, you should look for clues which give you guidance about how you should structure your answer and for warnings about things to avoid.

EXAMPLE:

In some plays, from the very beginning, the seeds of destruction of characters or institutions can be detected.

Show, by close reference to the text, how the opening section of any play you know well alerts the audience to the possibility of destruction to come.

Do:

✔ Establish which "characters" or "institutions" you intend to discuss. Most people would choose characters here. Obviously, these will have to be characters whose lives do follow a downward spiral, ending in failure or death.

✔ Define what is meant by "seeds of destruction".

✔ Clarify in your own mind what these "seeds of destruction" are that lead to the downfall of the characters.

✔ Identify how these factors are present in the opening section of the play.

Don't:

✘ *Interpret this too narrowly by confining yourself to the first scene.* The question refers to the "opening section" of the play. In a five-act tragedy by Shakespeare, for instance, it would be sensible to interpret "opening section" as the whole of Act One.

✘ *Overlook the second part of the question.* The other danger is that the whole essay will not go beyond the first act. The words ". . . alerts the audience to the possibility of destruction to come" allow, and expect, you to widen out your discussion to cover the whole play.

FOR PRACTICE

Look at these sample questions taken from past Higher papers. Try to identify what guidance in the wording of the questions is offered to help you work out what you should do and what you should not do. (It would be suitable to try this during class in pairs or in small groups). At this stage, you do not even need to think of a particular text to write about: just try to develop the habit of analysing the wording of the question itself. Begin by asking yourself: "what are the key words in this question?" Pick them out and try to define what they mean.

1. "The abiding genius of Shakespeare is that he gives us characters about whom we care." By referring in detail to the actions and language of one character in a play by Shakespeare, explain to what extent you agree with the above comment.

2. "After hundreds of thousands of novels and short stories, there can be no new stories any more, only different treatments of the same broad themes . . ." With reference to any novel or short story, show how, though the theme might have been familiar to you, the novel or short story nevertheless led you to new insights.

3. Choose a novel or short story whose structure is based on a journey or a quest. Show how the writer makes use of this structure to develop character or theme. (The journey or quest can be literal or metaphorical).

4. Many memorable poems leave the reader with a powerful impression of a person, a place, or an era. Using a poem which has left you with such an impression, explain what techniques are used by the poet to convey this impression.

5. What characters actually do; what characters say; what other characters say about them — there are many ways by which a playwright can create a character. From a play or plays which you have studied, examine the techniques the author has used to make a character or characters convincing.

6. Choose a play which explores the status of women in society and show to what extent they are seen as victims or as dominant figures.

Stage Two:
Planning the Essay

Once you have clarified in your mind what the question is asking you to do, you should make some preliminary notes before you start writing. It is tempting not to bother doing this, particularly when working to a time limit in a class assessment or in the exam. But a few minutes planning your essay *will* save you wasting time later on.

Before you start writing your essay, you should have a clear idea of how it is going to develop. If you **don't** plan it out first, you'll probably run into one of the following difficulties:

✗ you remember a point later on that you wish you had raised earlier;

✗ you mention all the things that first come to mind and then realise that you don't know what to say next;

✗ you state in your introduction that you are going to follow a certain line but, as you haven't planned it out in advance, your discussion gradually moves further away from your original aim.

Planning need not take more than about five minutes. You don't have to write anything out in detail; the briefest of headings will do. Your final draft, or course, should be neatly presented and laid out. Your planning notes, however, are only for your eyes and might well be rather messy, with bits scored out and arrows used to change the order of the points. In fact, your planning notes *should* look like this: if you make all your changes at the planning stage, you won't have to make so many when you write up the actual essay.

On pages 18–23 you will be shown how to plan an essay on "Macbeth"; on pages 32–34 there is a similar plan for an essay on a short story called "The Bike"; and on pages 42–43 there is guidance on writing an essay on the poem "To a Mouse".

Stage Three:
Beginning the Essay

Now that you have a clear outline of the essay in mind, you are ready to begin writing the introductory paragraph. You should focus on the **question** right from the very first sentence: don't take a roundabout approach such as giving a short account of the story. You should summarise the line of argument that you intend to follow in the essay.

EXAMPLE (1):

Here is a possible opening paragraph for essay question 1 on page 7, based on Shakespeare's *Hamlet*. The question reads as follows:

> *"The abiding genius of Shakespeare is that he gives us characters about whom we care."*
> *By referring in detail to the actions and language of one character in a play by Shakespeare, explain to what extent you agree with the above comment.*

> A character in a Shakespearean play about whom we care is Hamlet. We sympathise with him because of the difficult situation he finds himself in after his father's death, particularly with his need to seek revenge on Claudius. The fact that Shakespeare uses frequent soliloquies to give us an insight into Hamlet's thinking helps us to see things from Hamlet's perspective and further increases our involvement with him.

Notice that

- the opening paragraph should be short and general in its approach; it is too early in the essay to get into detailed discussion of individual points. The introduction should, in effect, be a summary of the whole essay.

- the question referred to the "actions and language" of the character. This means that both the content of the play and the style of writing should be considered. The introductory paragraph touches on both these aspects: the difficult situation Hamlet finds himself in ("actions") and the use of soliloquies ("language").

EXAMPLE (2):

This is an introductory paragraph for question 3 (page 8), based on Graham Greene's novel, *The Third Man*, which tells the story of a novelist called Rollo Martins who sets out to discover the truth behind the death of his friend Harry Lime in post-war Vienna.

The question reads as follows:

> *Choose a novel or short story whose structure is based on a journey or a quest.*

> *Show how the writer makes use of this structure to develop character or theme. (The journey or quest can be literal or metaphorical).*

A novel whose structure is based on a quest is *The Third Man* by Graham Greene. The quest takes the form of the central character, Rollo Martins, searching for the truth behind the death of his friend Harry Lime, in the course of which the reader not only finds out more about the personalities of Martins and Lime but learns something about the themes of friendship and betrayal.

Notice how this paragraph goes straight to the aspects referred to in the question, making reference to the key words of "quest", "character" and "theme."

FOR PRACTICE

Write similar introductory paragraphs for a selection of the other sample questions on pages 7–8 or for questions in your book of past papers, based on any text you are familiar with. Exchange your attempts with your partner and decide whether you each think the other's paragraphs are suitable.

Remember that a good introduction will:

- ✔ focus on the question straightaway;
- ✔ refer to key words from the question;
- ✔ give an outline of the argument presented in the rest of the essay.

Stage Four:
Developing the Essay

Planning the essay in a way which makes its relevance to the question clear is the most important thing in writing a critical essay.

Imagine the examiner was looking at two separate candidates' efforts. Writer A had planned his essay in a relevant way but had not included a great amount of detail from the text itself. Writer B knew her text really well and poured out a great deal of detailed knowledge. However, her essay never really got down to answering the question.

Neither of these answers would be ideal, of course, but writer A is likely to score a rather better mark than writer B. The candidate who manages *both* aspects — relevance to the question plus detailed knowledge of the text — will score much more highly.

Backing up your points with evidence

The basic principle that you should follow in each paragraph of your essay is simply: **back up what you say with evidence from the text**. Evidence from the text will usually take one of two forms:

- a reference to a scene, event or conversation which you summarise in your own words
  (paraphrase)

- a direct use of actual words from the text
  (quotation)

A convenient format here is: **generalisation — evidence — comment**. In other words, state the point you wish to make, back it up with a paraphrase or quotation, and then comment on what exactly this evidence reveals about your point. What you must avoid doing at this stage of essay writing is simply retelling the story of *what happens*. Select only the parts of the text which are directly relevant to the topic of the essay.

EXAMPLE:

At the start of the play, Macbeth is at the height of his reputation as a military leader. For example, he is described as "brave Macbeth", "worthy gentleman" and "Bellona's bridegroom". These descriptions emphasise that Macbeth's military skills are such that it is almost as if he is "married" to Bellona, Roman goddess of war.

[generalisation]
[evidence]
[comment]

FOR PRACTICE

Here are three exercises to give you practice in writing detailed paragraph units. They refer to well-known works of literature, but you do not have to have read these in order to complete the exercises.

1. *A Christmas Carol* by Charles Dickens

This short novel is about the transformation of the main character, Scrooge, from being a cold-hearted miser into a kind and generous uncle and employer. Imagine that you are writing an essay on the change in Scrooge's character. In one paragraph you set out to provide evidence of his meanness at the start of the book. From your reading you have noted down several relevant quotations from Dickens' description of him:

"a squeezing, wrenching, grasping, scraping, clutching, covetous old sinner."

"The cold within him froze his old features".

You have also noted plenty of examples of his meanness:

he only has a very small fire in his office, even although it is December;

the fire in his clerk's room is "so very much smaller that it looked like one coal";

when his nephew comes to wish him a merry Christmas, he says "Bah! Humbug!";

when two charitable gentlemen ask him for a donation to help the poor he refuses and says that it would be better to allow the poor to die and "decrease the surplus population";

when carol-singers come to his door he chases them away;

he grudges giving his clerk (Bob Cratchit) a holiday on Christmas Day.

WHAT YOU HAVE TO DO

Use this material to write a paragraph on the **generalisation — evidence — comment** pattern. (There is enough here to back up your point with several examples, although you do not need to use all this information.)

Begin your paragraph with the following topic sentence:

Dickens presents Scrooge as a mean and grasping person.

2. *Tam O'Shanter* by Robert Burns

This famous poem tells of how Tam, having drunk too much, allows his curiosity to get the better of him as he passes "Alloway's auld haunted kirk" while riding home. The whole subject is treated by the poet in a humorous and ironic way. Again, here is a selection of comments and quotations on this topic, listed in no particular order.

Irony is when the writer really means the opposite of what he says.

Much of the humour of this poem is based on irony.

Burns pretends to warn Tam that he should have listened to his wife and stayed at home instead of going out drinking but this warning is not meant to be taken seriously.

Some of the poem's humour comes from the use of Scots dialect.

At the end of the poem Tam doesn't suffer — his horse does, but Burns pretends to draw a serious moral from the story and advises Tam to learn a lesson.

Useful quotations:

"O Tam! had'st thou but been sae wise,
As ta'en thy ain wife Kate's advice!"

"Ah gentle dames! it gars me greet*
To think how monie counsels sweet,
How monie lengthen'd, sage advices
The husband frae the wife despises!"
                    [* i.e., makes me weep]

"She taught thee weel thou was a skellum.
A blethering, blustering, drunken blellum."
                    [refers to the way Tam's wife tells him off]

"Whene'er to drink ye are inclined . . .
Think! ye may buy the joys o'er dear,
Remember Tam O'Shanter's mare."

WHAT YOU HAVE TO DO

Using the above material, construct a paragraph on the **generalisation — evidence — comment** pattern, discussing the subject of the poem's humorous style.

Begin your paragraph with the following topic sentence:

Burns uses a variety of methods to create humour in "Tam O'Shanter".

3. **The Withered Arm by Thomas Hardy**

This short story tells of a milkmaid called Rhoda Brook who had a child by a farmer who then married someone else. Rhoda has many unhappy experiences: she is accused of harming the young wife by witchcraft, and witnesses the hanging of her own son. Here is the final section of the story:

> For some time she could not be found; but eventually she reappeared in her old parish, — absolutely refusing, however, to have anything to do with the provision made for her. Her monotonous milking at the dairy was resumed, and followed for many long years, till her form became bent, and her once abundant dark hair white and worn away at the forehead — perhaps by long pressure against the cows. Here, sometimes, those who knew her experiences would stand and observe her, and wonder what sombre thoughts were beating inside that impassive, wrinkled brow, to the rhythm of the alternating milk-streams.

WHAT YOU HAVE TO DO

Write a paragraph on the **generalisation** — **evidence** — **comment** pattern, showing how at the end of the story the sufferings of Rhoda Brook have left permanent effects on her, physically, emotionally, socially, etc. Remember that your evidence can take the form of paraphrasing as well as direct quotation.

Begin your paragraph with the following topic sentence:

At the end of "The Withered Arm" we are aware that Rhoda Brook's sufferings have left permanent effects on her in a number of ways.

4. **Michael by William Wordsworth**

Michael is a fairly long narrative poem by the nineteenth century poet William Wordsworth, who lived in and wrote about the Lake District in the North West of England. Michael is an old shepherd who had hoped to pass on his farm to his son Luke. However, the family falls on hard times and Luke has to go away to seek work in the city. What keeps Michael going is the hope that he will return and continue to look after the sheep. This extract describes the old father saying farewell to his son. Michael promises to continue working on a sheepfold which they had been building together.

> Then, pointing to the stones near which they stood,
> Thus, after a short silence he [Michael] resumed:
> "This was a work for us; and now, my son,
> It is a work for me. But, lay one stone —
> Here, lay it for me, Luke, with thine own hands.

Nay, Boy, be of good hope; — we both may live
To see a better day. At eighty-four
I am strong and hale; — do thou thy part;
I will do mine. I will begin again
With many tasks that were resigned to thee:
Up to the heights, and in among the storms,
Will I without thee go again, and do
All works which I was wont to do alone
Before I knew thy face . . . Now, fare thee well —
When thou return'st, thou in this place wilt see
A work which is not here: a covenant
'Twill be between us; but, whatever fate
Befall thee, I shall love thee to the last,
And bear my memory with me to the grave."

WHAT YOU HAVE TO DO

- First, discuss what this extract shows about the relationship of father and son — in particular, Michael's love for Luke. Look up the meaning of the word "covenant" and work out what this tells us about the relationship. The technique of **symbolism** is used here. Find out what this term means, and discuss how the building of the sheepfold is used in a symbolic way.

- Once you have understood these points, write a paragraph on the **generalisation — evidence — comment** pattern in which you discuss both the relationship of Michael and Luke and the techniques that William Wordsworth uses to explain this relationship to the reader.

This time construct your own topic sentence.

Stage Five:
Ending the essay

Sometimes an essay loses marks because it seems to end abruptly or have no proper conclusion.

The word "conclusion" means two things:

- an ending;

- a judgment, following logically from an argument.

The last paragraph of your essay should combine both senses of the word. It should:

- recap briefly on the main points;

- refer to the words of the question;

- sum up clearly and logically, drawing together all the threads of the argument.

Try to avoid mere repetition of what you have already said; there should be a clear sense of progression and development towards your conclusion. This can be achieved by adding one last, pertinent point, or by ranking your arguments in order of importance. Always make sure you have provided a genuine and relevant answer to the question.

EXAMPLE:

Here is a possible concluding paragraph for the essay on the question of Hamlet being a character we care about:

> It is therefore because we sympathise with Hamlet's predicament that we "care" about him throughout the play. We feel sorry for him because of the loss of his father, because he feels betrayed by his mother and because he finds himself having to take on the corruption within the Danish court almost single-handedly. He accepts dutifully, but unwillingly, the role of avenger, leading inevitably to his death. Our feelings for Hamlet are made stronger because we are given so many insights into his inner agony through his frequent soliloquies. We share in Ophelia's lament, "O what a noble mind is here o'erthrown". Perhaps most of all we are moved by this sense of waste, expressed also in Fortinbras' tribute to the dead prince, whom, he felt, would have proved "most royal" had destiny not prevented him from ever becoming king. As the play ends on this note of regret, it is clear that Shakespeare's genius has indeed been "to make us care".

CHECKLIST

In this chapter we have seen how to:

   read the question;
       look out for clues in the wording of the question which will help you structure your answer.

   plan the essay;
       divide the question into sections and make a list of paragraph headings which relate to these.

   begin the essay;
       use words from the question and introduce the main aspects you are going to examine in depth later.

   develop the essay;
       *use detailed evidence from the text, following the **generalisation — evidence — comment** pattern.*

   end the essay;
       sum up your main points, arriving at a logical conclusion, and refer back to the key words of the question.

The end product

This chapter has explained the *theory* of writing a critical essay. It has given you some practice in writing *parts* of an essay but we now have to apply this method to writing a complete answer.

The next two chapters will provide two worked examples which go through the five stages of essay writing and end up with complete sample essays.

The first example is on Shakespeare's *Macbeth*. If you are studying this text in school, the sample essay provided will help you with your coursework (although if you copy it out and try to pass it off as your own work your teacher is bound to notice!).

If you are not studying the play in class, a second example is given, based on a Scottish short story, *The Bike*, by Fred Urquhart. The text of this story is printed in full, and some preliminary notes and questions are provided before this material is worked into the form of a critical essay.

II : *Writing an essay on 'Macbeth'*

Stage one:
Reading the question

Do you sympathise with Macbeth or do you feel that he deserved everything that happened to him?

Make sure you understand what the question is asking you to do:

- Both sides of the question should be considered: how far you sympathise and how far you feel he deserved his fate. Your answer could therefore be organised around a "FOR" and "AGAINST" approach.

Stage two:
Planning the essay

Divide a sheet of paper into two columns. Head the first column "FOR" and the second one "AGAINST". In the first column, list all the reasons you can think of for sympathising with Macbeth. In the second, list all the reasons for feeling that he deserved what happened to him.

This stage could be done in class, working in pairs or groups.

FOR   AGAINST

Next, draw up a paragraph plan, such as the following:

Paragraph One:
   Introduction, outlining the topic to be discussed and making reference to key words
   from the question.

Paragraph Two:
   Discussion of some of the ways in which you sympathise with Macbeth (FOR):
      e.g., his good qualities as shown in the earlier part of the play; his bravery and
      loyalty in the battle; his wife's description of him as being "full of the milk of
      human kindness"; the fact that he does have a sense of right and wrong, etc.

Paragraph Three:
   Discussion of further aspects which lead us to sympathise with him (FOR):
      e.g., the way that he is tempted by the witches and persuaded by his wife (see
      Act One, Scene Seven, in particular).

Paragraph Four:
   Discussion of how Macbeth is nevertheless responsible for his own actions
   (AGAINST):
      e.g., contrast between how Macbeth and Banquo react to hearing the witches'
      prophecies. How his selfish ambition is made clear early on.

Paragraph Five:
    Discussion of how Macbeth alienates our sympathies by suppressing his feelings of guilt and how he commits further evil acts (orders murder of Banquo, Macduff's family, etc.) (AGAINST).

Paragraph Six:
    Conclusion.

Drawing up such a plan will mean that you do most of your thinking at the planning stage. When you start writing the essay, you will have a clear idea of its overall shape.

Stage three:
Beginning the essay

Remember that the introduction should be short and general in its approach, summarising the main points which the essay will develop. It should immediately focus on the words of the question. A possible opening for this essay might be:

At the start of Shakespeare's tragedy "Macbeth", the protagonist has a reputation for heroism; by the last act he is described as a "dead butcher". It is certainly true that we sympathise with Macbeth at first, particularly because of the way in which he is influenced by the witches and Lady Macbeth. Nevertheless, as the play progresses, we ultimately recognise that he has to be held responsible for what happens to him.

Stage four:
Developing the essay

What follows is a sample essay in which the points listed under the paragraph plan at stage two are developed by providing detailed evidence from the play. Notice how the pattern of **generalisation** — **evidence** — **comment** is used here.

- Each paragraph begins with a topic sentence outlining the main idea which the rest of the paragraph expands in more detail.

- Linking words and phrases are used to help the essay to flow and to make logical connections between points.

- An element of personal response is included.

The notes down the left hand side are designed to draw your attention to these features when they occur in the course of the essay.

Do you sympathise with Macbeth or do you feel that he deserved everything that happened to him?

Introductory paragraph stating what the essay is going to discuss.

At the start of Shakespeare's tragedy "Macbeth", the protagonist has a reputation for heroism; by the last act he is described as a "dead butcher". It is true that we sympathise with Macbeth at first, particularly because of the way he is influenced by the witches and Lady Macbeth. Nevertheless, as the play progresses, we ultimately recognise that he has to be held responsible for what happens to him.

Topic sentence

Evidence to back up main point

Further evidence, linked to previous point by a connecting phrase ("More significantly")

There were certainly times in the play when we feel inclined to take Macbeth's side. Early on, for instance, his admirable qualities are particularly apparent. It is he who saves Scotland during the battle, which leads him to be praised as "brave Macbeth", "worthy gentleman" and "Bellona's bridegroom". More significantly, he is rewarded by King Duncan for his loyalty and bravery by being given the title of the traitor Cawdor — and, of course, the lands that go with the title. Even Lady Macbeth's criticisms of her husband in a way provide evidence of his good nature, such as when she describes him as "too full of the milk of human kindness."

Topic sentence. Note that the words "In addition to his own attributes . . ." link back to the previous paragraph and take the argument a stage further

Evidence and quotations backing up main point

In addition to his own attributes, we feel sympathetic towards Macbeth because of the temptations and influences to which he was subjected. The witches hail him as "king hereafter", and his wife reinforces this suggestion by manipulating him into hastening the fulfilment of the prophecy himself. She makes the murder a test of his love for her — "from this time / such I account thy love" — and, in spite of his recent triumph on the battlefield, accuses him of being afraid to act to secure the crown:

"Woulds't thou have that
Which thou esteemst the ornament of life
And live a coward in thy own esteem?"

The cleverest approach of all is to steer the discussion away from *whether* he should kill Duncan to *how* he might do the deed. We cannot but sympathise with Macbeth at the end of the first act. He tells his wife "I am settled" but adds "false face must hide what the false heart doth know", showing that he knows he is acting against his better judgment.

Linking phrase "in spite of all this" indicates a change in the line of argument.

In spite of all this, Macbeth must still be held responsible for his own actions and ultimately does deserve his fate. While it is true that the witches hold out a tempting prospect to him, he could have resisted the temptation. There is a noticeable difference between Macbeth's immediate acceptance of the prophecies —

>"Glamis, and thane of Cawdor!
>The greatest is behind!"

— and his friend Banquo's more cautious approach:

>"oftentimes . . . to win us to our harm
>the instruments of darkness tell us truths."

Macbeth's reaction here amply demonstrates that the selfish ambition to be king was already in his mind, and even at this early stage the idea of murdering Duncan occurs to him, although as yet the thought is but "fantastical".

Again, the words "Most of all, however" link back to the previous stage of the argument and point forward to the next stage.

Most of all, however, Macbeth alienates our sympathies by deliberately suppressing his conscience. His tragedy is that he did not start the play as a "butcher": he had a moral sense which made him fully aware when he was doing wrong. The reader does sympathise with his inner torment after the murder and with his spiritual alienation when he says that he could not say "Amen" when Duncan's guards prayed "God bless us". We understand his agony that "All great Neptune's ocean" cannot "wash this blood clean from my hand" — but we also recognise that he suppresses his feelings of guilt and continues to commit further atrocities such as having Banquo murdered, believing that he is

>"in blood
>Stepp'd in so far that . . .
>Returning were as tedious as go o'er"

When we hear that Macduff's wife and child — who are no direct threat — have been slaughtered and we learn that "each new morn new widows howl", Macbeth forfeits any

Personal response

right to our sympathies. He becomes so inhuman that his only reaction to the death of his wife — to whom he was previously so close — is "she should have died hereafter." By the end of the play he has lost the will to live and life has become merely

>"a tale
>Told by an idiot, full of sound and fury,
>Signifying nothing."

Stage five:
Ending the essay

The concluding paragraph should sum up the main arguments and present your final judgment, including the "key words" of the question.

Repeat key word "sympathy"

Macbeth's heroic defiance in the final battle reminds us poignantly of the noble figure he presented in the opening battle scenes. However, by the time he dies at the hands of Macduff, it is impossible to respond with sympathy. During the course of the play, Macbeth's conduct has become progressively more ruthless and devious. While acknowledging that he was subjected to powerful temptation, we feel that ultimately he has consciously aligned himself with the "instruments of darkness" and thus

Repeat key phrase "deserve . . . him"

he does indeed "deserve everything that happens to him".

How good is it?

A good essay must meet all the "performance criteria": understanding, analysis, evaluation and expression.

✔ *The essay has to show that the writer has a secure **understanding** of the text.*
   The essay contains plenty of detailed references and examples. It shows a sound understanding of the play's theme: how a character with potential to be great is destroyed through ambition.

✔ *The essay has to contain detailed **analysis** of the writer's technique.*
   The question was about character development rather than techniques such as imagery, word choice, etc., and this answer clearly analyses the stages of Macbeth's downfall.

✔ *The essay must also demonstrate **evaluation** of the ideas discussed.*
   This means that it is not enough simply to trace the stages of Macbeth's downfall in a factual or narrative way: there has to be awareness of how important various factors were in causing this outcome, and the candidate has to use his judgment in assessing these factors. The essay achieves this by indicating how the audience's sympathies change as the play goes on.

✔ *The **expression** of the essay has to be sound.*
   This example makes use of connecting phrases to direct the flow of the argument and has clear topic sentences at the start of paragraphs which make everything relevant to the question. There is also appropriate use of personal response ("I felt sympathetic because . . .", etc.) while a suitably formal and analytical tone is maintained throughout.

III : *Writing an Essay*
on a
Short Story:
"The Bike" by Fred Urquhart

Preliminary study

Although it is set in the 1920s or 1930s, this story is based on a theme which is familiar to everyone: the choice we all have to make between spending money on the small pleasures of life or sacrificing these to save up for something special. You might like spending money on magazines, CDs, visits to the cinema, and so on; at other times you begin to think "if I cut down on the small luxuries I could have a better holiday or even start saving for a car . . ."

In this Scottish short story by Fred Urquhart, the main character, Annie, is a girl who works in a wine merchants. She has very little spare cash but is determined to save up for a bicycle of her own.

THE BIKE

Fred Urquhart (b. 1912)

The bicycle cost her seven pounds ten. It took her almost three years to save the amount. She did without the pictures and new stockings and sweets and lots of other things to get it. The other girls in the wash-house laughed at her determination to save. When they sent Tammy for pies and ice-cream and lemonade they always tried to coax her to get some, too. And they laughed at her refusals and said she was mean. They could not understand her desire to have a bike.

'What dae ye want a bike for, onyway?' Lizzie the forewoman said. 'What guid's it goin' to dae ye?'"

'I don't know,' Annie said. 'I just want a bike.'

She could not put into words her longing to sail along superbly, skimming like a yacht in full sail. The only argument she could find in its favour was that it would save car fares. 'It costs me fourpence a day to get here,' she said. 'I'd save that if I cycled. Five fourpences and twopence on Saturdays. What's that?'

'Guidness knows,' Lizzie said. 'I never was ony guid at coontin'.'

'Twenty-two pennies,' Annie said, her brows wrinkled with the effort of calculation. 'That's one and — one and tenpence.'

'Ay, it's a guid bit oot o' ten bob a week,' Lizzie said.

'Well, it's time we got on! Harry's yellin' aboot thae Domingo Souza bottles no' bein' labelled yet.'

Still, although the other girls in the wine and spirit merchant's warehouse saw that Annie's reasons for wanting a bicycle were good, it did not prevent them from jeering at her for saving. They said she was a mug not to get it on the instalment system. Annie refused to do that, however. It was too much like getting a thing "on tick". And so she saved and dreamed. Dreamed of the time when she would be able to dash along freely without feeling crushed on the crowded pavements.

But the three years were long when she saw the number of pies the other girls consumed and the bottles of lemonade they tilted to their dry mouths. Sometimes she thought it wasn't worth it: the bike seemed as far away as ever. And she would look at the little penny bank-book that was all that she had to show for her scrimping, and she thought often of blowing the whole amount on a new coat or on a trip to Blackpool. But she sternly set her mind against the temptations that the other girls whispered to her. And at last she got her bike.

It was a lovely bike. A low racer, painted a bright red, with cold gleaming chromium-plated handle-bars. The first morning she passed her hand proudly over its shining mudguards before she jumped upon it and whisked along to her work. She wouldn't need to steal any more rides on her brother's bike! Here was something of her own: something she could clean and oil and tend; something she could keep shining and spruce. Her heart sang with exhilaration and proud accomplishment, keeping time with her feet working the pedals and the wheels going round. She had a bike! *Oh, Georgia's got a moon, and I have got a bike! The one I've waited for, and I have got a bike!* And she waved gaily as she passed Lizzie and Meg and Bessie walking to the warehouse.

She put the bike behind the barrels at the back of the washhouse. It was safely out of the way there.

Everybody in the warehouse came to admire it. 'It's a nice wee bike,' said one of the lorry-drivers. 'Ye look real smart on it. I saw ye wheech past the tram-car I was on this morning, and I said to masel, "Is that Annie?" Ay, ye're a real smarter!'

'What did ye say ye paid for it?' asked Charlie, the youngest lorry-driver.

'Seven pounds ten,' Annie said shyly.

'Oh boy!' Charlie whistled with astonishment. 'Some capitalist made a pile out o' that. Ye were a mug to encourage him. Fools and their money!'

Charlie was always talking about the capitalists and about wage-slaves and socialism and the revolution. He was a loud-voiced, swaggering young man, rather good-looking in a flashy sort of way. Although he was never properly shaved and always wore a muffler instead of a collar and tie, Annie was very much attracted by him. But he never encouraged her either by look or by word, and she was too shy to show that she liked him.

That afternoon as Annie returned to work she overtook Charlie at the gate of the warehouse. She jumped off her bike and walked with him towards the wash-house.

'Ay, it's a nice bike,' he said, eyeing it critically. 'How much did ye say ye paid for it again?'

'Seven pounds ten.'

Charlie whistled tunelessly. He slouched along with his hands in his pockets. At the door of the wash-house he made no move to leave her. He leaned against the door-post. Annie stood, holding the bike, watching him, admiring the yellow curls that dangled over his low brown forehead.

'Seen that picter at the Gaiety?' Charlie said.

Annie shook her head. She caressed the bike's leather seat.

'Like to see it?'

'I was goin' tonight,' she said.

'Yourself?'

'Uhuh.'

'Mind if I chum you?'

'Okay,' she said.

All afternoon Annie could hardly work for thinking about going to the pictures with Charlie. Even the bike was overshadowed by this wonderful happening. She could hardly take her tea for thinking of what lay ahead, and she was at the corner of Commercial Street ten minutes before the time.

She hardly recognized Charlie when he mooched up to her with his hands in his pockets. He was wearing a collar and tie and a scarlet pullover, and his bright yellow hair was neatly arranged into waves like corrugated iron. It looked as though it had just been marcelled.

'Oke,' he said, balancing himself on his sharp-pointed shoes on the edge of the pavement.

Annie smiled. She pranced along proudly at his side in the direction of the Gaiety. She tried to think of something to say, but she could think of nothing. Charlie kept his eyes on the pavement, a cigarette dangling from his lips.

At the pay-box Annie fumbled in her bag. 'It's okay,' Charlie said, 'I'll get it again.' And he bent down to the bowl and said: 'Two sixpennies.'

The Pathé Gazette was showing. Annie was not much interested in soldiers marching and in naval reviews. She looked sideways at Charlie. He was slumped down in his seat, his hands in his pockets. Annie admired his profile in the semi-darkness.

The feature started. It was a torrid romance. Annie placed her hand on her knee close to Charlie's leg. He made no response for a long time. Annie could not enjoy the film for wondering why not. Then about the end of the film Charlie placed his hand over hers. But he took it away when the lights went up.

They said nothing as they walked to Annie's house. She slipped her hand through his arm, but he never took his hands out of his pockets.

'Well, I'll see you tomorrow,' he said at the door of the tenement. 'Cheerio!'

'Cheerio!' Annie said.

At first Annie kept the bike in the wash-house, but the foreman advised her to keep it elsewhere. 'Ye'd better watch it doesnie get scratched here, lass,' he said. 'If I was you, I'd put it in the garage. It would be safer there.'

But Annie discovered that the bike was not as safe in the garage as it had been in the wash-house under her own eye. The boys in the office and the two louts who looked after the yard were always racing it around the yard. She began to notice marks on the paint, and sometimes when she went to get it she found that the seat had been raised.

'If I was you, I'd tell thae galoots where they got off,' Lizzie said. 'Especially that lazy brute, James. It would be wiser-like if he helped puir Tammy to sweep up the yard instead o' racin' roond and roond.'

But James did not heed Lizzie when she gave him a flyting. 'Awa' and mind yer ain business,' he said.

And he continued to cycle madly around the yard whenever Harry, the foreman, was out of the way, leaving Tammy, a simple-looking youth of about seventeen, to do all the work.

Annie would have brought the bike back into the washhouse but they got in an extra lot of barrels and there was no room for it. Sometimes she thought that she would be better to leave the bike at home and take the tram to work as she used to do. But although she was now getting twelve and sixpence a week she could not afford anything from it for tram fares. She went to the pictures once a week with Charlie and she always paid herself. Lately, too, they had taken to going to dances, which meant spending one and sixpence or two shillings which she could ill afford.

Apart from her dislike of James for using her bike, she disliked him for his influence on Charlie. They were as thick as thieves. Every night after work they went into the public house at the end of the street although already they had drunk all the wine and whisky they could scrounge from the warehouse. 'I'd like to see their insides,' Lizzie said. 'They'll be bonnie and burned!'

Whenever Charlie had too much drink he talked about 'the capitalists grinding the faces of the poor', and there were always several adjectives describing the capitalists. But he had so great a capacity for drink that it was difficult to tell when he had had too much. Annie hated to see him at those times, though she was fascinated and could not help listening to what he was saying. She was terrified that he would drink too much at the dances they went to and cause her to feel embarrassed.

One forenoon six or seven weeks after Annie had bought the bicycle, Charlie was in such a state that even the foreman remarked upon it. 'He's awa' oot as fu' as a puggy,' he said to Lizzie. 'And him wi' a load o' stuff on his lorry that's worth thoosands. I hope he's able to deliver it a', and that nothin' happens to him.'

But Charlie was able to deliver all his orders safely at the various pubs and licensed grocers. He returned to the warehouse about five o'clock, and his lorry swung into the yard far too quickly for the amount of space available.

'That yin'll kill somebody yin o' thae days, if he's no' carefu',' said Lizzie, looking out of the wash-house.

'He's needin' taken doon a peg,' Bessie said, wiping her red hands on her packsheet apron and scowling over Lizzie's shoulder at the boastful Charlie as he swung empty boxes and crates from his lorry on to the ground. 'I havenie forgotten aboot what he did to the puir cat.'

This had happened some time before. The cat was a great favourite with everybody in the warehouse except Charlie. It was a good ratter, and when it was about, the girls weren't afraid to plunge their hands into the straw in the crates: they knew there was no danger of rats lurking there when Towser was about.

But one day Charlie had swung his lorry into the yard and headed straight for the cat, which was lying stretched out in the sun. Somebody had noticed and cried a warning. But Charlie had taken no notice, and the wheels had gone right over the animal. And when Lizzie and Bessie had lashed him furiously with their tongues, Charlie had laughed and said: 'The beast had no right to be lying there.'

'He'll get an awfu' drop yin o' thae days', Bessie muttered now. 'I only hope I'm there when he gets it.'

'Me too,' said Meg.

'Lookit the way he's chuckin' the boxes doon and leavin' them lyin' for puir Tammy to put in their places,' Lizzie said.

'That's a socialist for ye,' Bessie said.

'Thae kind that talk sae big aboot their socialism are aye the worst,' Lizzie said.

Annie felt that she should champion Charlie, but she could think of nothing to say. She continued to wind pink tissue wrappers around bottles of Lodestar Ruby Wine.

Having thrown off every box and crate, Charlie jumped into the driving-seat and started his lorry. He headed straight for the garage door. 'He'll run into it if he doesnie look oot', Lizzie said.

But he managed to scrape through. 'That was a near thing,' Lizzie said, turning and picking up a crate of empty bottles.

Just then there was a crash. It was not very loud, but it was loud enough for the sound to be unfamiliar. 'What's that?' Bessie cried.

The four girls ran into the yard. Harry had already run out of the office, and some of the young clerks were following him. They approached the garage door.

Charlie met them. He was grinning broadly. 'It's okay,' he said.

'What was that noise?' Harry said.

'That!' Charlie shrugged. 'That was just that lassie's bike. What did she need to leave it for in the middle o' the garage?'

Numbly Annie stared at the twisted wheels and the broken red frame. She scarcely heard the arguments that went on around her. Dimly she heard Lizzie shriek: 'That's that James goin' and leavin' it lyin' there in the middle o' the floor!' And even more dimly she heard Charlie reply: 'D'ye think I'm lookin' oot for every heap o' scrap-iron that's in my way?'

That night Annie cried herself to sleep. Harry had assured her that she would get a new bike. 'I'll make Charlie and James pay it between them,' he promised her. 'Charlie can rant as much as he likes about the insurance being liable, but I'll see that he pays for it.'

But Annie knew that even if she got another bike it would never be the same. She would always remember Charlie's derisive grin as he looked down at the broken frame, and his scornful words. She knew that something more than her bike had been broken. Nothing would ever be the same again.

© *Fred Urquhart*

In the pages which follow, you will see how this story could be used as the basis for a critical essay. Before planning and writing the essay, however, it will be helpful to examine various aspects in detail. As with most texts, the main areas to look at are the following:

Setting
Plot
Characters
Themes
Style and technique.

Each of these aspects will be looked at in turn; points marked ● contain questions for you to consider. These can be done in writing or could form the basis of classroom discussion.

1. Setting

(i) *Political Background*

The historical and geographical background of this story are both relevant to the character development and themes. The story takes place in an industrial town in Scotland somewhere between the Russian Revolution of 1917 and the General Strike of 1926. This was a time of social unrest when poverty was widespread, strikes were frequent and the trade union movement was strong in the West of Scotland which gained the nickname "red Clydeside" as a result. Prominent political figures at this time were the Labour Member of Parliament James Maxton and the union leader and pacifist John McLean. Political meetings were common and the character of Charlie in the story has clearly attended these and has been influenced by some of the socialist and communist ideas which were popular at the time among the working classes.

● Quote some of Charlie's remarks which show this.

● Quote a remark from one of his workmates which reveals rather less enthusiasm for Charlie's political views.

(ii) *Details of ordinary life*

Another aspect of the story which helps to locate it in a particular time and place is the descriptive detail relating to everyday life at work and at leisure.

● Make a list of the details mentioned that are typical of ordinary life at the time and which are not so familiar today.

2. *Plot*

While it is important to remember that you should not simply retell the story in a critical essay, you should nevertheless have a clear idea of the plot in your mind.

● Try to write a straightforward summary of what happens in this story, either in note form or in a few paragraphs of connected prose. (It is not necessary to use quotations here).

3. *Characters*

There are only two major characters: Annie and Charlie. We'll look at them separately and then examine how their relationship develops.

Annie

● The story begins by emphasising how much she wants the bike and stresses how many obstacles she had to overcome before she achieved her ambition. Make a list of FIVE of the difficulties she has to face.

● Quote some words which describe the appearance of Annie's new bike.

● Write down TWO aspects of owning the bike that bring her particular pleasure.

● Which words suggest how happy she is at having achieved her aim?

Charlie

● Think of two or three adjectives which would sum up the personality and appearance of Charlie.

● Find an example or quotation to back up each of these.

● What do you think Annie finds attractive in Charlie?

● What indications are there (earlier in the story) that Charlie is also a dangerous character for Annie to become involved with?

The relationship of Annie and Charlie

● When does Charlie first take notice of Annie? Do you think there is any significance in this?

● How does Charlie behave when he is going out with Annie? In what ways does Annie seem concerned about how things are going?

● How does the relationship come to an end? Looking back, do you think Charlie had been planning such an ending right from the start?

4. Theme

The main theme or idea running through this story could be described as disillusionment: Annie hopes that both the ownership of the bike and her friendship with Charlie will bring her happiness, but neither turns out as she had hoped.

● How does the author bring these two ambitions — the bike and Charlie — together at the end?

The last sentence *"Nothing would ever be the same again"* also applies both to the bike and to future relationships with people.

● What has Annie now learnt about human nature? How will this affect her in the future?

A number of different techniques are used effectively to convey the theme of disillusionment:

5. Style and technique

(i) *Symbolism* is used in the last paragraph — i.e., when something stands for something of wider significance. In this case, the broken frame of the bike symbolises Annie's broken heart.

(ii) *Structure*: A closer examination of the story in the light of the concluding paragraph will show that certain links between Annie's feelings about the bike and her feelings about Charlie had already been hinted at earlier. The author skilfully keeps this point until the very end so that we only realise in retrospect (that is, looking back) that the bike and Charlie had been linked all the way through.

● In both cases, Annie has to wait before she gets what she wants. She has to save and sacrifice for the bike, while *"Charlie never encouraged her by look or by word."*

● The bike is described as *"a low racer, painted a bright red, with cold gleaming chromium plated handle-bars"*; Charlie is described as *"good looking in a flashy sort of way"* and wears *"a scarlet pullover"* on their first date.

● When Annie got her bike *"her heart sang with exhilaration and proud accomplishment"*; when she went out with Charlie at first *"she pranced along proudly at his side"*.

(iii) *Dialect* is another technique of interest. The way the people speak adds to the realism of the story's period setting.

● Quote some examples

Note that dialect and slang expressions are constantly developing and some of the phrases used in the story have fallen out of use. For example, when the foreman tells Lizzie that Charlie is *"awa oot as fu' as a puggy"* he is using an expression popular in the railway industry for which the Glasgow area was once famous. A "puggy" was a nickname for a small steam locomotive used for shunting duties.

● Look at some examples of how Charlie speaks to Annie. Does this tell us anything about their relationship?

Writing the essay

You should now have a good understanding of the setting, plot, characters, themes, style and technique of "The Bike". But even if you memorised and reproduced all that material word for word it would still not be an acceptable essay answer. In this section, we will apply the method of essay writing explained in Section One to the preliminary work on "The Bike" which you have just completed. The structure of this section will be similar to the previous one on "Macbeth", with this difference: instead of being shown a sample essay at the end, you will be asked to write one yourself.

<h1 align="center">Stage one:
Reading the question</h1>

Here are a number of questions on short stories from past papers.

1.   Short story writers cannot afford to waste time on unnecessary detail. Considering one short story, show how the choice of significant detail is used to increase your understanding of character, plot and theme.

2.   Often the setting of a prose work takes on an importance beyond that of simply providing the characters with a background against which to act out their lives. In any prose work which you have studied, show the importance of the writer's use of setting in the portrayal of character and / or action.

3.   Isolation, rejection, confrontation or loneliness are major themes that are explored in many novels and short stories. By examining the techniques used by an author, show how one of these themes is dealt with in a way which you found meaningful.

4.   Discuss any Scottish prose work — novel or short story — which in your opinion deserves recognition not only in Scotland but elsewhere. What features of this work seem to you to be particularly Scottish and what features should give it a more universal appeal?

5.   The novelist Robin Jenkins has written that "fiction ought to create credible characters, in situations that are moving and in some way illuminating." How well does a short story you have studied fit this description?

FOR PRACTICE

In groups or pairs, discuss the wording of each of these questions.
- Make sure that you see exactly what the question is asking you to do.
- Is any guidance offered about how the essay could be structured?
- Which parts of the questions would students be most likely to overlook or misunderstand?
- Which aspects of "The Bike" would be particularly relevant to these questions?

Stage two:
Planning the essay

Question 5 above would be particularly well suited to "The Bike". In discussing its wording, you may have noticed that this question implies a discussion of three different aspects:
- how the characters are credible, i.e., what makes them seem like real people;
- what makes the situation "moving", i.e., why we sympathise with the problems faced by the characters;
- why the situation is "illuminating", i.e., what it teaches us about human nature.

FOR PRACTICE

Working on your own, or with other pupils, make notes under the three headings: 'credible', 'moving', 'illuminating'.

Stage three:
Beginning the essay

Now write an opening paragraph for this essay. If necessary, look back to pages 9–10 and model your answer on the format used there. Remember that in your introduction you should:
- ✔ identify the title and author of the story;
- ✔ use words from the question;
- ✔ mention the aspects you intend to discuss in the rest of the essay (in this case characters and situation);
- ✔ avoid including detail or examples but simply take a general overview of the question.

Stage four:
Developing the essay

Expand your outline notes into a full length essay, by backing up your comments with quotations, following the **generalisation** — **evidence** — **comment** pattern which was practised in the last two chapters.

Remember that at the start of every paragraph you should look back to your introduction to check that you are still on course and that you have not veered off in some other direction. Do not begin your paragraphs with detailed points but with general topic sentences, often referring back to the specific words of the question.

Look at these two sentences as possible openings for a paragraph:

(1)   *Annie decided not to buy a new coat or go on a trip to Blackpool.*

While this may be a perfectly true statement about the character, it is not a suitable opening sentence in an essay. It simply makes one detailed point and does not give the reader any clue about how the paragraph will develop. Nor does it have any direct connection with the question.

(2)   *I felt Annie was a credible character because I could understand how difficult it must have been for her to resist the various temptations that confronted her.*

This is much better: it refers directly to the question ("credible character"); it makes a general point (Annie was faced with temptations) which will lead into detailed examples in the rest of the paragraph; it includes some personal response ("I could understand"). Try to begin your paragraphs in this way.

Stage five:
Ending the essay

Return to the point you started with in your introductory paragraph and summarise what you have proved in the course of your essay. While you will be referring back to points previously mentioned, try to vary your word choice so that it does not sound repetitive. Use synonyms.

How good is it?

When you have finished your essay, don't neglect the all important checking stage. You could use the following as a checklist which covers what the examiners are assessing under the performance criterion "expression".

✔ Are there any spelling mistakes?

> *You will know what particular words have caused you trouble in the past. For instance, it may be words with double letters like* disappearing. *It is a good idea to keep a page at the back of your folder where you list the words you tend to spell wrongly.*

✔ Is the punctuation correct?

> *In particular, check that you have not run two sentences together with a comma instead of a full stop, a common fault sometimes known as the "comma splice".*

> *Use a colon (:) to introduce a quotation.*

Avoid a common error!

Note that 'however' and 'therefore' are adverbs, not conjunctions. They should not be used to link clauses. Usually these words should follow a semi-colon or a full stop rather than a comma.

For example:

✔ At the opening of the play we are drawn to Macbeth because of his courage; **however**, by the end we despise him for his ruthlessness.

✗ At the opening of the play we are drawn to Macbeth because of his courage, **however** by the end we despise him for his ruthlessness.

✔ Have you used linking words and phrases to signpost the direction of the argument?

> *These are essentially of four different kinds:*

> (i) ***Adding on a similar point:*** *useful words and phrases here are*
> *furthermore;*
> *moreover;*
> *in addition to this;*
> *similarly.*

(ii) *Making a different point from the previous one:* useful words here are
> however;
> nevertheless;
> on the other hand;
> in contrast to this.

(iii) *Placing ideas in order of importance:* useful words here are
> in particular;
> more importantly;
> of greatest significance;
> above all.

(iv) *Drawing a conclusion:* useful words here are
> thus;
> therefore;
> as a result of this;
> consequently.

✔ Have you used quotations?

Quotations should not be longer than one or two lines. Don't include quotations for their own sake: quote only enough to back up the point you are making.

✔ Have you used quotations properly?

*Make sure your quotations really do **illustrate** a point and don't just **repeat** that point. Don't write this kind of thing:*

> Annie made sacrifices to save up for a bike.
> She did not go to the pictures and did not buy
> stockings, sweets or other luxuries.
>> "She did without the pictures and
> new stockings and sweets and lots of other things
> to get it."

Why do you think this is not a worthwhile use of a quotation?

You should also make sure you don't simply string a list of quotations together with brief comments in between.

✔ Have you used a suitable tone?

While it is acceptable to use the first person "I" as this helps to make your essay come across as a personal response to the text, you should not write in an informal way. Do not use shortened forms (don't, can't, and so on); do not use abbreviations (such as etc. and e.g.) and, of course, avoid slang expressions.

✔ Have you shown awareness of the terminology of literary criticism?

> *You should be able to write about things like: literal and metaphorical language; imagery; symbolism; irony; tone; conflict; themes; climax and anti-climax; narrative viewpoint; jargon; dialect; persona, and many other similar terms.*
>
> *[For more on the vocabulary of literary criticism, see Part Three of this book which deals with the Personal Study].*

✔ Is your essay properly structured?

> *Even if it does have an introduction and a conclusion and it does make reference to the question, your essay should be structured as an **argument** with each step leading to the next in a logical way. Weaker essays are often structured as a **list** of separate points.*

✔ Does the content of your essay meet the "understanding, analysis and evaluation" criteria?

> *Your **understanding** of the text will come through in your use of detailed evidence from the text, and in your selection of relevant quotations to back up your statements.*
>
> *Your **analysis** will show that you are aware of how the author's use of literary techniques contributes to our understanding of the theme. In this case, the technique of symbolism is particularly important.*
>
> *Your **evaluation** of the story will come through if your essay does not just concentrate on the plot of the story but shows that the plot helps to convey something about character development and gives insight into aspects of human nature. The aspects of human nature in this case might be ambition, determination, envy, trust, destructiveness, naïvety, disillusionment, rejection and so on.*

Remember that the "understanding, analysis and evaluation" performance criteria should not be approached in a mechanical way — in other words, don't try to write a paragraph showing your understanding of the story, a paragraph dealing with an analysis and so on. Your fulfilment of these criteria will come through in the essay as a whole.

IV : *Writing an Essay on a Poem:*
"To a Mouse"
by
Robert Burns

Several times during his short life (1759–1791) Robert Burns tried to scrape a living as a farmer, with little success. Once, while working in a field he accidentally disturbed the nest of a mouse. This led him to consider that, as a poor farmer struggling to keep a roof over his head, he had quite a few things in common with the small, defenceless creature. The famous poem *To a Mouse* was written as a result. In a way, it can be seen as an early literary statement about animal rights.

*On turning her up in her nest, with the plough,
November, 1785.*

WEE, sleeket, cowran, tim'rous beastie,
  O, what a panic's in thy breastie!
Thou need na start awa sae hasty,
      Wi' bickering brattle*!   * *rapid scamper*
I wad be laith to rin an' chase thee,
      Wi' murdering pattle*!   * *spade-like tool for cleaning plough*

  I'm truly sorry Man's dominion
Has broken Nature's social union,
An' justifies that ill opinion,
      Which makes thee startle,
At me, thy poor, earth-born companion,
      An' fellow mortal !

  I doubt na, whyles*, but thou may thieve,   * *sometimes*
What then? poor beastie, thou maun live!
A daimen-icker in a thrave*   * *in other words, an occasional ear of corn*
      'S a sma' request:
I'll get a blessing wi' the lave*,   * *the rest*
      And never miss't!

Thy wee-bit housie, too, in ruin!
Its silly wa's the win's are strewin!
An' neathing, now, to big a new ane,
          O' foggage* green!   ** coarse grass*
An' bleak December's winds ensuin,
          Baith snell* an' keen!   ** bitter*

   Thou saw the fields laid bare an' wast,
An' weary Winter comin fast,
An' cozie here, beneath the blast,
          Thou thought to dwell,
Till crash! the cruel coulter* past   ** blade of the plough*
          Out thro' thy cell.

   That wee-bit heap o' leaves an' stibble*,   ** stubble*
Has cost thee mony a weary nibble!
Now thou's turn'd out, for a' thy trouble,
          But house or hald,
To thole* the Winter's sleety dribble,   ** endure*
          An' cranreuch* cauld!   ** hoar frost (i.e., white frost on the ground after*
                                             a cold night)

   But Mousie, thou art no thy-lane,
In proving foresight may be vain:
The best laid schemes o' Mice an' Men,
          Gang aft agley*,   ** wrong*
An' lea'e us nought but grief an' pain,
          For promis'd joy!

   Still, thou are blest, compar'd wi' me!
The present only toucheth thee:
But, Och! I backward cast my e'e,
          On prospects drear!
An' forward, tho' I canna see,
          I guess an' fear!

Taking a closer look

As with most poems, *To a Mouse* can be examined from the point of view of the ideas it contains (content) and the language techniques used (style). The following questions will help you achieve a closer understanding of the text. They can either be used for written answers or as the basis of group discussion. Ensure you write full notes on each topic, as this material will later be reworked into an essay on the poem.

1.   **Burns's feelings about the mouse**
     (a)   What is the mouse frightened of in verse one?
     (b)   How does the poet try to reassure the mouse?
     (c)   For what does he apologise in verse two? What do you take *nature's social union* to
           be?

(d) Write down **three** ways in which he says that he is like the mouse (from verse two).

(e) What has the mouse been guilty of doing (verse three)?

(f) How does the poet excuse this?

(g) What disaster overcomes the mouse in verses 4–5?

(h) What troubles will the mouse now have to face (verse 6)?

In the last two verses Burns compares himself to the mouse.

(i) In what ways are their problems in life similar?

(j) How is the mouse more fortunate?

Did you know . . . ?

- over half the households in Britain today own a pet.

- the RSPCA estimates that there are around half a million stray dogs roaming the streets of Britain.

---

2. **The language of the poem**

Burns is famous for his skill in putting the Scots dialect into poetic form. This is done very effectively in this poem in various ways. Where appropriate, find quotations as evidence of the following points:

(a) *Dialect creates a conversational effect.*
It is as if the poet is actually speaking to the mouse.
- Quote **two** separate lines which show this.

(b) *Dialect is used to show Burns's sympathy for the mouse*
The fact that he bothers to speak to it shows that he cares about what is going to happen to the creature and he tries to see life from its point of view.
- Quote **four** separate lines or phrases which show this.

(c) *Dialect is useful for sound effects.*

Look, for example, at the description of the winter weather in verses 5 and 6. The hard, grating vowel sounds of 'cranreuch cauld' [frost] effectively convey the harsh winter conditions that the homeless mouse will have to endure.
- Comment on the sound effects of

  'Till crash! The cruel coulter past
                    Out thro' thy cell.

What figures of speech are used here?

(d) *Dialect reinforces the message of the poem*

The poem uses a simple style of language and rhyme scheme, as it deals with the simple, basic necessities of life. It is not notable for its use of figures of speech; the language is factual and literal as it deals with ordinary, down-to-earth things: the daily struggle for food, shelter and warmth.

● Quote some lines which refer to such basic everyday aspects of life that are as important for people as they are for animals

(e) *There is a mixture of dialect and standard English*

You may have noticed that verse two is written in a different style from the rest of the poem.

All the other verses have a local setting; verse two has a universal application.

The other verses are *particular* — one specific man in a field talking to one mouse — whereas verse two is *general*.

What Burns is saying here was quite radical in his time: he is apologising on behalf of the human race for its treatment of its fellow-creatures. 'Nature's social union' is the notion that man and animal are made to live in harmony, but this harmony had been broken by man exploiting and mistreating animals.

Burns's thinking here was an influence on the poets of the Romantic Movement, such as William Wordsworth (1770–1850) whose favourite subject was nature in the widest sense of the word — from a small flower to the landscapes of the Lake District. (See, for example, the extract from *Michael* on pages 14–15).

Did you know . . . ?
As a result of stricter controls and higher standards of animal welfare, the number of experiments carried out on animals for research purposes has halved in the last twenty years.

Writing the Essay

Stage one: Reading the question

Here are a number of questions on poetry from past papers.

1. Choose a poem which has something important to say to you. By closely referring to the poet's language, briefly explain why you consider the subject matter to be important, and go on to analyse how the language conveys the importance of the subject.

2. Some poets succeed in presenting fresh and unusual insights by using everyday speech patterns and vocabulary. Their work may, for example, include the use of cliché, or informal expressions or idioms. Examine the work of a poet who may be described in this way and explain how he / she succeeds in providing the reader with new insights. (You may deal with one or more than one poem in your answer).

3. Many poems are concerned with a sense of loss or sadness at a particular event. Examine the means by which a poet, in one such poem, conveys either of these emotions to you.

    You should, where relevant, refer to such features as rhythm, rhyme, word choice, language, sound, imagery, symbolism, style and structure.

Stage two: Planning the essay

The rest of this section will show you how to prepare an answer to question 1 above.

●   Make notes on the 'something important' that the poem has to say to you.

●   Identify two or three main language techniques.

●   Find examples of these **and** discuss why they are effective. Remember to follow the **generalisation — evidence — comment** pattern.

●   Think why the technique is suitable — i.e., how does a particular technique help the reader to understand the message of the poem better?

●   Write down a paragraph plan, so that you know roughly what you are going to discuss in each paragraph **before** you start writing the essay.

Stage three: Beginning the essay

Here is a sample introduction to the question we are looking at:

> *A poem which had something important to say to me was 'To a Mouse' by Robert Burns. Working in a field in the winter, the poet accidentally destroys the nest built by a mouse and this leads him to consider the hardships faced by animals and how these are not so different from the difficulties facing humans. Burns's use of Scots to convey this message makes the poem particularly effective.*

●   Judging by this introduction, which aspects of the poem are going to be discussed in the rest of the essay?

Stage four: Developing the essay

Each of the following sentences could be used as a topic sentence for a paragraph in the essay. Note that in each case the sentence links back to the question and points forward to what the rest of the paragraph will discuss.

●   Using these sentences as the openings for your paragraphs, continue writing the essay. Where you see a row of dots, you should add your own detailed discussion of the poem, including quotations.

The important message that Burns wants to convey in this poem is one of sympathy for the mouse . . .

However, Burns's point does not simply concern one particular mouse, but has a more universal application . . . [discuss verse two here].

A further important aspect of what the poet has to say in this poem is that the human race should show more concern for animals as both man and beast have similar needs in life . . .

Burns's message is made all the more effective because of the language he uses . . . [write two or three detailed paragraphs developing this point, drawing on the work you have just completed on the effects achieved through the use of the Scots dialect].

Stage five: Ending the essay

Round off the essay with a concluding paragraph which refers back to the question and summarises the main points you have covered in the essay.

Finally, check over the essay for spelling and punctuation errors, and go through the 'How good is it?' checklist on page 23.

PART TWO

Writing in a Particular Genre

Writing in a Particular Genre

"Writing's simple. You take out a pen and jot down the first thing that occurs.
The writing is easy; it's the occurring that's difficult."
(Stephen Leacock, (1869–1944), Canadian writer and Professor of Economics)

WHAT YOU WILL BE ASKED TO DO

You will be asked to compose a piece of original writing. In the case of certain genres, such as persuasive or argumentative writing, you may have to do a certain amount of research to ascertain facts, but it is important that the end result is unquestionably your own work.

WHAT THE EXAMINER IS LOOKING FOR

Content: This refers to the quality and depth of your ideas. The best writing will show insight and imagination. Expressive writing should be logical, clear and convincing; fiction should be gripping.

Structure: The structure selected should be appropriate for the purpose. Arguments should have an introduction and progress logically to a conclusion; stories should generally have a beginning, middle and end.

Expression: Your style should also be appropriate for the type of writing: personal / reflective writing might be chatty and colloquial in tone, whereas a discursive essay is likely to be more formal; sentence structure should be fluent and varied and word choice effective. Whatever style you choose, you must communicate clearly.

Technical Accuracy: This includes grammar, spelling, punctuation and paragraphing. You should check and edit your work carefully to achieve a high degree of technical accuracy. Examiners and teachers are very familiar with 'careless' errors which include the omission of words, the repetition of words or mistakes in the use of capital letters.

Beware of the spell-checker!

Spell-checks on computers and word-processors are useful tools which help if you are unsure about the form of a word, such as whether or not it may contain a double letter. They can also detect misprints such as 'nad' for 'and'. However, the spell-check cannot help you decide between 'there' and 'their' or 'know' and 'now'. You must not assume that your work will be perfect just because it has been spell-checked.

Always read it through.

PLANNING AND DRAFTING

Planning is important whatever type of writing you choose to do.

A useful type of plan which is simple, yet works well in practice, is the "spider" diagram. This involves drawing a circle into which you write your topic. You can then draw "legs" from the body of the "spider", annotating them with the ideas or stages in your essay. You should start at the top and work round in a clockwise direction.

Here is an example of how a spider plan for an argumentative essay on capital punishment might look. To show how the plan would grow it has been drawn in two stages. The boxes with a solid outline are the first ideas that were thought of and those with a dotted outline were added later. It is easy to fit in ideas which you think of later, as you simply add another "leg" to the spider at an appropriate and logical place.

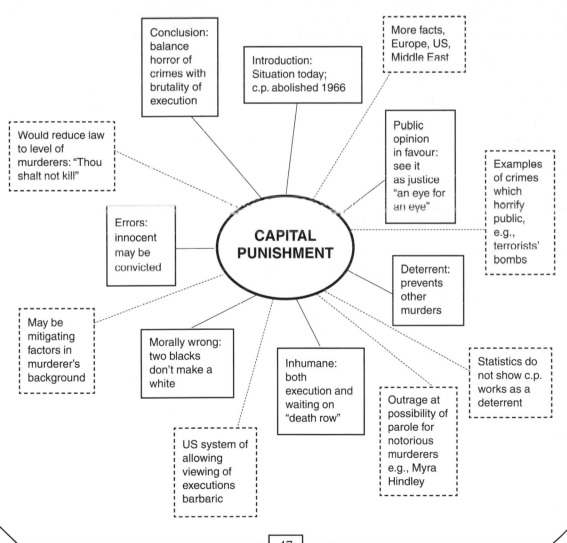

WRITING IN A PARTICULAR GENRE

With a partner, devise a "spider" diagram on any non-fiction topic of your choice.

An alternative type of plan is to arrange your ideas in a list, taking a new line for each. There is an example of this type of plan in the section on reflective writing on page 61.

Don't forget . . .

Evidence

Keep your earlier drafts. Some examination boards have a rule that earlier plans and drafts of any written work must be available as proof that the work is all your own.

Length

Always check with your teacher or tutor whether your course has particular regulations with respect to length. There may be either a maximum or a minimum word limit. Generally, it is advisable not to submit a piece of writing which is excessively long. It should be possible to demonstrate your skills in around 1000 words. On the other hand, a very short piece (under 650 words) may come across as 'thin'.

Presentation

Clear presentation will enhance your work. Many institutions now have rules that submitted work must be word-processed, and you should aim to do this if possible. Use a plain font such as Times. Avoid elaborate fonts such as those which imitate handwriting, as examiners find them hard to read. The font size should be 12 or 14 point and you should use double spacing between the lines. If you have to write by hand, use a black or dark blue pen, and write on one side of the paper only. Try to use clean, good quality paper. Make sure all pages are numbered and stapled firmly together in the right order.

Redrafting

After drawing up your plan, you should then write a first draft. The next stage is to pass it to your teacher or tutor to read and comment on it. Additionally, or alternatively, you might exchange your piece of writing with a partner: you can comment on each other's work, and suggest any possible changes which might strengthen the impact of it.

It is not necessary to accept all the suggestions you are offered, but generally a second opinion is helpful in order to discover if your aims in the piece of writing have succeeded or not. Sometimes merely by leaving it for a few days and returning to it, you yourself will see where changes might be made.

In a second draft you should

- Try to develop strengths, eliminate weak areas, and possibly do some rearranging of your material.
- You should make an effort to polish up your expression and eliminate all technical errors. Consult a dictionary, if necessary. Computer spell-checks are helpful, but they must always be used with caution.
- Read over your finished work carefully, even if you have used a spell-checker.

WHAT SHOULD YOU WRITE ABOUT?

Your English course will require you to compose a piece of writing in a particular genre.

A "**genre**" is a type of writing. There are **six** basic options to choose from. To help you make up your mind, the different types are classed into two groups as follows:

Group A: **Expressive**

1. Personal / reflective
2. Persuasive
3. Argumentative

Group B: **Creative**

4. Prose fiction (e.g., short story, chapter of a novel)
5. Poem, or a set of thematically linked poems
6. A dramatic script (e.g., scene, monologue, sketch)

The next few pages will explain each of these genres in more detail, and provide some samples of writing by both professional writers and students for you to analyse. In the section, "Finding a Context", you will find some advice on how to select a topic of your own.

An important rule is that your writing must be "**entirely your own work**".

"**Plagiarism**" is the term given to copying someone else's writing and passing it off as your own. It is natural, and indeed desirable, that you will try to imitate the practices of writers whose work you admire. However, you must imitate their *practices*, not their *work*.

Do **not** attempt to use the plot of a film or TV programme you have seen as the basis for a piece of writing. This is also a form of plagiarism.

"**Parody**". It is acceptable — although not necessarily easy! — to produce a *parody* of another type of writing. A "parody" is a humorous imitation of another writer's work. A story about a secret agent whose name is James Bone, and whose boss's secretary is Miss Honeypenny would be clearly seen as a parody of Ian Fleming's spy stories: this is very different from copying one of Fleming's plots and pretending you have thought of it yourself. To be on the safe side, you should include a question or task statement which makes it clear: e.g.,

> ## Produce a piece of writing in the style of . . .

Reminder:

You should keep your plan and earlier drafts. These may have to be checked as proof that the work is authentically your own.

Genre 1: Reflective / personal writing

Essentially, a reflective essay is an attempt to explore some aspect of the world, presented in a way which will interest or give pleasure to the reader. It should have the effect of prompting the reader to think and perhaps compare his or her own views on the subject with yours.

WHAT THE EXAMINER IS LOOKING FOR

A sense of your own **personality**: appealing traits are modesty and enthusiasm.

Expression of your **thoughts and feelings**, not just a narrative account.

An **entertaining treatment** of the topic; originality and perhaps humour.

Appropriate **style**. A chatty one may be more suitable than a formal one. Remember, however, that a conversational style must be controlled with careful and accurate punctuation.

Although the terms **personal** and **reflective** are linked within this category, either element may be focused upon, but each aspect must be included. Thus, an essay which focuses on yourself must include reflection, while a reflective essay must show a personal viewpoint. It is worthwhile repeating the warning from the Higher English Unit Notes:

Reminder:

> **"The reflective essay at Higher (or Intermediate II) is *not* simply an account of an experience."**

PERSONAL WRITING

The following two extracts are from essays written by school pupils. Each was on the very common topic of *Myself, as I see Myself*, and presents an impression of the writer and the writer's parents. Each writer also says something of the relationship between the two generations. In groups, discuss the questions which follow the two extracts.

Extract 1: Stephen's essay

"Huffy" was the word most commonly used to describe me in my earlier years. As a small, helpless, handsome, angelic looking boy, I found it necessary to be able to fight back against the god-like, remote, even at times, rather frightening figures, more commonly known as my parents. The tantrum, which consisted mainly of screaming and bawling, was a means of gaining attention and, to an extent, power. The huff was the more subtle option, and was frequently used to baffle my parents about the cause of the problem.

Now that I am almost seventeen years old, a new, more sophisticated development of the "huff" is still occasionally applied. However, I can now solve problems diplomatically and can even genuinely accept refusal. Perhaps I am actually becoming more like my parents? The thought which seemed impossible during my earlier years may now be coming horribly true.

Extract 2: Kirsty's essay

> Over the last few years I think I have grown up
> considerably.
>
> I have taken on responsibility both in and out of
> home. During the holidays I help my mother with
> the housework, by doing the hoovering, dusting,
> ironing and washing the dishes. I also help with
> the animals as I have three ponies, a dog and a
> cat which involves an awful lot of work. When I
> was younger, I absolutely hated doing the
> housework or working in the stable. I used to
> think my parents moaned at me too much. But, now
> that I have grown up I realise how much work my
> mother and father must have to do, and I think
> that I should at least help them when they have
> had a hard day at work.

1. Compare the opening sentences of each essay. Comment on the effectiveness of each as an opening.

2. Each writer goes on to present a picture of him / herself as a child. Pick out expressions or details which are likely to engage the reader's interest. Which is the more appealing?

3. Compare the way the two writers portray their early relationship with their parents. Pick out expressions and comment on how the relationship is put over in each case.

4. Look at each writer's view of how they have changed over the years. What does each writer convey about his / her personality?

5. Compare any other features of style which seem to you noteworthy in any way. You might mention tone, vocabulary or sentence structure.

6. Give each writer a mark out of 10, giving reasons for your grading.

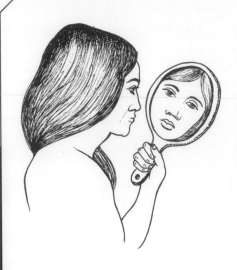

The topic of "Myself" is totally focused on personal experience. Some of the examples you will be given in the *Finding a Context* section (pages 91–93) are also very personal — describing a relationship that has gone wrong, for example. Personal essays often score very well, as each person's experiences are unique, and so you can be sure of writing something original. However, while the experiences themselves may be unique, you must be careful that your responses and reflections are carefully and precisely worked out, and are not mere clichés.

REFLECTIVE WRITING

A more demanding type of writing is the reflective essay where you present your thoughts on a topic which is not simply part of your own experience. You might choose a topic of social concern. Here the reflective essay may seem to overlap with the argumentative or persuasive type (choices 2 and 3). However, an essay *will* be reflective if it focuses largely on *your* response to the topic, rather than on the topic itself. You might, for example, explore the world of teenage magazines in a humorous and entertaining way, although the same topic could be used for a serious discussion. Very often a topic will be more abstract, such as "happiness".

The range to choose from is very wide. A selection of topics chosen by a fifth year class included the following:

Growing Up	Education
War	Family Life
Superstition	Social Class
Friendship	Fear
Beauty	Balancing Two Cultures
Foretelling the Future	Sport
Money	Power
Racism	Love

The following extract is from a pupil's essay on the topic of "Laughter".

Jennifer's essay

An adult laughs on average forty-seven times a day. This statistic may be surprising to many, demonstrating that we are unaware of how much we do actually laugh. A giggle at an amusing comment made by a friend or a joke told on the radio is usually dismissed quickly and appears insignificant but these moments of joy are in fact extremely important in our lives. The most satisfying aspect of laughter is that it is something which is generally shared, between friends or family or perhaps, most surprisingly, between strangers. It is surely amazing that two people who know nothing about each other can be linked momentarily by the intimacy of laughter.

One of the most spirit lifting sounds is that of children's laughter. It encapsulates a sense of freedom and innocence which cannot fail to awaken memories of one's own childhood. Although it may be difficult to back up scientifically, I feel that there certainly is some truth in the old cliché "laughter is the best medicine", as it is hard to find something which compares to the feeling of being convulsed with laughter until your mouth aches and tears roll down your cheeks.

How far do you feel Jennifer fulfils the four requirements of reflective writing which were outlined on page 51?

Very good examples of reflective writing are to be found in the work of regular columnists in quality newspapers. It is strongly recommended that you read these from time to time as they will provide excellent models of good practice — as well as an enjoyable read. A textual analysis of one of these pieces of writing will show how a professional writer successfully entertains his readers. This example is by Ian Wood, golf columnist of *The Scotsman*.

It's a sore point but if there's no pain there's no gain.

During a recent news report on television, some schoolteachers in England, who had just won millions of pounds in the Lottery, were featured and one of the group was asked how she felt about it. "Gobsmacked", she replied. What poetry, what effortless mastery of the lingo. As Prime Minister Tony Blair has said so often: "education, education, education". It is, indeed, a
5   boon and a blessing.

Had there been a lottery when I was at school and some teachers had won it, it is difficult to imagine any of them saying he or she was gobsmacked. Not that the word existed then, but if it had, it almost certainly would have been frowned upon.

Of course, there's no telling how even the most severely correct teachers would react on learning
10 that their ship had just come home, laden to the gunnels. The sense of responsibility which drives such people might well become blurred as they begin to realise that on the morrow — or even earlier — they can bid farewell forever to the whey-faced little creeps they've been stuck with all this time.

Very probably, the gobsmacked teacher on television was already mentally far away, heading for
15 the Bahamas or getting up the noses of her neighbours by roaring around in a brand-new Ferrari or one of the vast four-wheel-drive efforts I see billowing about these days, equipped with the bull bars which are so essential when it comes to picking your way through the thundering herds of bison which range freely in the Morningside* area of Edinburgh.

It may be that the best thing about the Lottery is thinking about winning it, for experience shows
20 that the reality rarely lives up to the dream. I often muse about buying top-of-the-range, state-of-the-art golf equipment which will help me roll back the years.

*   Morningside is a residential suburb of Edinburgh.

Not that there's that much to roll back from, for there wasn't a lot there in the first place, but I
live in hope that somehow the hidden reserves of power I know are in there dying to get out
will be released one day by some potent combination of graphite and titanium which I haven't,
25 as yet, come across.

Deep down, though, I know it will never be as simple as that and that any golfing success I'm
likely to achieve now will involve pain and plenty of it. This grim message was driven home just
before Christmas when I was setting out early on a cold, crisp morning to play at Gullane.
Striding purposefully from the house, I stepped on to a sheet of black ice and went into the sort of
30 routine which is normally accompanied by Ravel's *Bolero*.

One of the drawbacks of the more mature frame is that it loses its bounceability, that resilience
which is so marked in early life and which enables people to dust themselves down and
swagger off whistling after walking into walls and falling from great heights. When I come to
earth these days, I find elasticity is almost totally absent. It is as if a medicine ball* has been
35 thrown on to a wet pavement.

Thus it was that I took some minutes to rise from where I lay, flat on my back, with one leg
buckled under me. Having gone through a kind of cockpit drill, checking that neck, fingers,
toes, undercarriage, etc., were all in working order, I rose and limped off to the golf course,
aware that a lump the size of a medium free-range egg had come up under my right knee-cap.

40 At the course, in the strange way that things work out in such situations, I found myself playing
with an old friend who'd had both hips replaced with plastic jobs. As the round wore on it
became evident that we didn't have a decent leg between us and our progress up the first hole
must have resembled something out of Napoleon's retreat from Moscow. Oddly enough,
though, walking and hitting the ball wasn't the problem. The problem was picking the ball out
45 of the hole after putting.

My partner had developed a technique which involved lowering himself by bending at the
knees, keeping his back erect and groping for the ball with his dangling arm. As I was unable
to bend my right leg, I opted for a method whereby, with the stiff leg held out side-ways as a
counter-balance, I hopped past the right-hand side of the hole using my left leg, which I could
50 still bend, to lose altitude, and attempted to scoop the ball out with my free hand as I
staggered by. A good deal of ducking and bobbing went on and it was all a bit like the courting
ritual of storks on an African game reserve.

The strange thing is that I played my best golf in a long time, which suggests that as far as my
game is concerned, the sorer the better. If that means hurling myself out of the house in the
55 mornings, then so be it.

* a medicine ball is a heavy metal weight.

QUESTIONS

Marks

(a) Structurally, this article falls into three main parts. Paragraphs 5 (lines 19–21) and 7 (lines 26–30) link the three sections.
   (i)   What is the main topic in each of the three parts of the article? **3**
   (ii) Show how paragraph 5 and paragraph 7 form links. **4**

(b) In paragraph one, the teacher who won the Lottery said she was "gobsmacked". Explain clearly why the writer was surprised at her choice of word. **2**

(c) (i) Comment on the tone of the sentence "what poetry . . . lingo" (line 3). **2**
   (ii) Which word in this sentence seems to belong to a different register from the rest, and what is the effect of this? **2**

(d) (i) What impression of schoolteachers is given by the phrases "frowned upon" (line 8) and "severely correct" (line 9)? **1**
   (ii) Explain how the phrase "whey-faced little creeps" (line 12) contrasts with this impression. **2**
   (iii) What is the tone of the writer's speculations in paragraph four (lines 14–18) on how the teachers will spend their lottery money? **1**

(e) Explain what the writer means by "the sort of routine . . . *Bolero*" (lines 29–30) **1**

(f) Look at the following expressions:
   "a kind of cockpit drill . . . working order" (lines 37–38);
   "something out of Napoleon's retreat from Moscow" (line 43);
   "a bit like the courting ritual . . . reserve" (lines 51–52).

   Explain how the writer gains his effect in any ONE of these phrases by the use of hyperbole (exaggeration). **2**

(g) The final paragraph contains the outcome of the writer's reflections : the "message" of the piece.
   (i) Explain the writer's "message" as it applies to this one incident. **2**
   (ii) Explain how the message might have a more universal significance, or how it might be applied more generally to a wider range of experiences. **2**

(h) One of the criteria of the reflective essay is that it should convey "a clear sense of the writer's personality". How does this writer convey his personality in each of the sections mentioned in question *(a)*? **6**

Total: 30

58

WRITING A REFLECTIVE ESSAY

Stage 1: Choosing a Topic

In groups, hold a "brainstorming" session in which you write down as many topics as you can think of. It might help to think of the themes of works of literature that you have studied.

A topic may occur to you spontaneously, or it may arise from a particular context.

Stage 2: Research

The next stage might be to do some research. Looking up a **dictionary definition** of your topic may trigger your thoughts. An **encyclopaedia** or other reference book may provide you with a surprising or unusual piece of information which might make a striking beginning or ending. This strategy was adopted by the writer of the essay on "Laughter" (page 55) with her statistic of forty-seven laughs a day. A **dictionary of quotations** may also provide a neat "sound-bite" on the topic and possibly start off some trains of thought.

Reflective essays lend themselves to showing off your knowledge a little. You can include references to films, TV, books, art or music to illustrate or elaborate on your thoughts.

Stage 3: Planning

In a good reflective essay the ideas will progress logically via a series of links to a satisfying conclusion. Avoid a mere series of disconnected thoughts. The most damning criticism is that such an essay seems "rambling". **Linkage** is your key. The following "list" method is a reliable way to plan a reflective essay. Alternatively you could use a "spider diagram" (see page 47).

A	Write down all your main ideas in a numbered list, taking a new line for each.
B	Group related ideas into four or more sections.
C	Arrange these sections into a logical order. Then, consider how each section may be linked with the next.
D	Devise an introduction and a conclusion. A description of a **scene**, or a **personal anecdote**, can provide a good opening; a **quotation**, or a **joke**, may provide a punchy ending. (Don't be discouraged if you find this part difficult: the beginning is often the hardest part. Instead, you could write the first draft, and consider adding or modifying the introduction later.)

Stage 4: Drafting

After writing your first draft, it can be very helpful to have a session in which you exchange your work with a partner. Without marking the draft, each of you should write down comments on the other's work on a separate piece of paper. If your work has been done on a word-processor, it is fairly easy to rearrange or alter it. If you are writing by hand, it is easier to wait until your teacher or tutor has also commented before redrafting.

Here, the research has been done for you, and the result is a "list" type of plan on the topic of "Christmas". Now, go through stages B, C and D of planning outlined above. First, arrange the ideas into related groups; then, arrange the groups into a logical order, and think of ways to link the various groups of ideas. Finally, consider which ideas you might use in the introduction and conclusion. You may, of course, add ideas of your own to this list.

1. *Dictionary definition: date when Christians celebrate the birth of Jesus.*
2. *Notes from encyclopaedia: Christian festival superimposed on earlier pagan festival of winter solstice, time of merrymaking, evergreen branches featured. Roman Saturnalia similar.*
3. *Santa Claus / Father Christmas myth.*
4. *Present-giving.*
5. *Shopping; Christmas rush.*
6. *Decorations.*
7. *Family gatherings.*
8. *Food: turkey, plum pudding, etc.*
9. *Commercialism criticised.*
10. *Cards.*
11. *Christmas trees.*
12. *Carols; cribs; nativity plays.*
13. *Political Correctness: Secularised in US.*
14. *Season of good-will.*
15. *Dickens's* A Christmas Carol; *Scrooge.*
16. *Loneliness; highest suicide rate.*
17. *Quotation: "We"ll keep our Christmas merry still": Walter Scott.*
18. *Entertainment: parties; pantomimes.*
19. *Expense: problems for poorer parents meeting children's expectations.*

Genre 2: Persuasive writing

If you feel you are not a very imaginative person and have trouble thinking up stories or describing feelings, you may prefer to try persuasive or argumentative writing. Essays of this kind are more likely to be factual in content and the organisation of the material will be one of the important things to consider.

Persuasive and argumentative writing are similar in some respects but they are not exactly the same.

PERSUASIVE WRITING

- Persuasive writing is when the writer puts forward a view and tries to persuade the reader to agree with it.
- It is basically one-sided.
- It may adopt a personal (i.e., subjective) stance.
- It can use a variety of tones to persuade the reader. It could, for instance, take a humorous approach.

EXAMPLE

In this article from *The Scotsman,* journalist Gareth McLean argues that among the young, television is losing out in popularity to the internet. This article could be seen as an effective piece of persuasive writing.

GARETH McLEAN ON WHY THE YOUNG ARE SWITCHING OFF

The article begins with an anecdote (i.e., a story to illustrate a point).

When the BBC unveiled its latest advertisement for "the unique way it's funded" as a schoolboy wandered through the landscape of children's television, it appealed to every grown-up's sense of nostalgia. From *Bill and Ben* to *Blue Peter* and *Bagpuss*, the Corporation unashamedly cashed in on our rose-tinted memories of listening to John Craven, hanging on Janet Ellis's every word and even hiding from the Daleks. The subtitles were subliminal: "Remember this? You wouldn't want the next generation to miss out on all this, would you? Of course you don't, so cough up your licence fee." And yes, it is the least us big people can do for "today's little people."

How does the point made in paragraph two contrast with paragraph one?

Only it seems today's little people aren't that interested in watching television any more. The one-eyed monster in the corner simultaneously charged with bringing violence and porn into our lives while also bringing the world into our living-rooms is having the plug pulled. As successive surveys show the decline in television audiences at its steepest among young people, it could be that it is not just programmes we will be feeling nostalgic for in years to come — it might be John Logie Baird's invention itself.

How does the tone of the article change here?

The downward trend in TV viewing, especially among young, educated professionals, can be attributed in part to the rise in popularity of the internet.

The author backs up his views by

(a) referring to statistics and

(b) quoting the opinions of experts.

Last year, a survey of 11,000 people by an Australian research company found that use of television fell by over half once people became internet users while American studies have shown similar results. And, according to author Don Tapscott, the next generation, today's little people, whom he dubs "the Net Generation", will abandon television even more quickly.

For what reasons does he think the young prefer their computers to television?

Note the use of a rhetorical question

(a)   to encourage readers to think what their own answer might be and

(b)   to lead on to the next stage of the argument.

How does the opening sentence of the last paragraph act as a topic sentence?

The author rounds off the article by returning to the lighter tone of the opening.

Under twenty years old, this generation embraces interactive media like the internet, CD-ROM and video games and are exceptionally curious, discriminating and more aware — technologically, globally — than any previous youth culture. They prefer interactive media to broadcast media, Tapscott maintains, and this is the reason they are watching TV less and less.

They favour the internet or PlayStation games because they are non-hierarchical and controllable. The Net Generation want to create their own stories, narratives, programmes in a way that is currently impossible on television.

So will the meteoric rise of the internet kill the television dinosaur? Rumours of its death may be slightly, if not greatly, exaggerated. Television is being forced to evolve by new technologies but its complete extinction seems unlikely.

Ironically, it's the BBC who are leading the way in harnessing the internet. Their website is one of the country's most visited and almost all of their programmes — from *Eastenders* to the news — have an internet site.

Other channels are also gearing up to use new technologies. Interactive broadcasting is being discussed by satellite and terrestrial channels and the advent of digital has opened up new horizons for the whole industry. In the next ten years, television will become more like the internet and vice versa. Television sets will effectively become computers and broadcasting companies will soon move into a high gear on the information superhighway — ABC, the American television network, has already taken over an internet search engine. As the Net Generation grows up, it looks increasingly more likely that we'll see a TV-PC hybrid develop and then we"ll have to learn how to deal with a whole new animal. For the moment, perhaps we should just savour the last days of a non-interactive *Blind Date* . . .

[Condensed from an article in *The Scotsman*, 18 March 1999]

Genre 3: Argumentative writing

- Argumentative writing is when the writer examines both sides of the question in a balanced way.
- It is likely to adopt a less personal stance (i.e., it is objective).
- It will probably use a formal, neutral tone.

FOR PRACTICE

This exercise can be done individually, in pairs or in groups.

1. *Think of a subject on which people hold widely differing views* — and preferably a subject on which you have a strong opinion too. Typical subjects might be: Is the media too powerful? Should drugs be legalised? Does television have a harmful influence on children? Is it better to be an only child or to have brothers and sisters? (Don't restrict yourself to these topics: they are just examples).

2. *Make a list of* all the various arguments on both sides of the question. Simply write them down in any order as they occur to you.

3. *Organise your arguments* in three stages:
   SORT them out into "FOR" and "AGAINST";
   GROUP related points together;
   RANK them in order of importance.

4. *Balance the arguments together and write down a conclusion that emerges from them.* For instance, you may discover that the arguments on one side are noticeably less convincing than on the other.

FOR PRACTICE 1

The outcome of this exercise will be an argumentative essay on the subject of the problem of increasing traffic congestion and what should be done about it. However, all the necessary points have been provided for you so that you can concentrate on organising the material and linking it into an argument.

Remember that each paragraph should begin with a general topic sentence showing that you are introducing a new stage of your argument. The column headed *Purpose* will give you a suggestion about what each topic sentence should say.

Paragraph	Purpose	Points to make
1	To introduce the topic under discussion and indicate the approach you are going to take in the rest of the essay.	Begin by referring to a recent RAC survey which revealed that the proportion of short journeys taken by car has doubled in the past twenty years. 20% of car journeys are seen as "absolutely necessary" but the other 80% are more a matter of choice.
2	To suggest why people prefer to go by car.	Convenience, privacy, security, lack of efficient alternatives . . . (Expand these ideas and add some others of your own.)
3	To show why this situation cannot continue.	In twenty-five years time, traffic is forecast to be double its present amount.

Back-up evidence: When the Forth Road Bridge was built thirty years ago, 4·5 million vehicles crossed it; figure is now 20 million. Possibility of building a second bridge is now being considered. |
| 4 | To consider some short-term measures that might reduce traffic growth. | Higher petrol duties might have an impact. Studies suggest that an increase of 10% in fuel prices could result in a 7% drop in petrol use. Government intends to raise fuel duties by 5% in real terms each year. |

BUT: this would be unpopular with motorists. May not work. Actual rise in pump prices has averaged less than 1% over the past three years because of weak oil prices and strong competition on forecourts.

5   To consider the expansion of some existing measures which might provide long-term solutions.

1.   More efficient public transport.

2.   Expansion of priority bus lanes on main routes (e.g., Edinburgh's greenways).

3.   Park and Ride schemes. Drivers leave their cars in car parks on the outskirts of the city and take a bus. This system has cut traffic in Oxford by 17%.

4.   Banning traffic altogether from city centres.

5.   Better town planning to help bring workplaces and schools within easy walking distance of home.

6.   Encouragement of cycling and provision of cycling lanes.

(These points are not necessarily in the best order. They will need to be linked rather than simply listed. Expand them with some of your own ideas as well.)

6   To draw conclusions from the points made in the rest of the essay.

A suitable way of rounding off your essay would be to use one of the following quotations from recent newspaper articles:

> *In the end, as drivers, we all need to ask ourselves, in the words of the old wartime poster, "Is your journey really necessary?"*
>
> *Perhaps it is time to start balancing the costs of convenience against the costs of doing nothing. And to make sure we include ourselves in the equation.*

FOR PRACTICE 2

The information that follows is on the topic of vivisection, the use of live animals in scientific experiments. It has been collected from five different sources. Source (i) is from material issued by the Biomedical Research Education Trust, a body which supports this use of animals; while source (ii) is from a pamphlet published by the British Union for the Abolition of Vivisection, which campaigns against it. Sources (iii) and (v) are extracts from a magazine article and a newspaper report. Source (iv) comprises two personal statements, one on each side of the argument.

TASK

Write an essay offering a balanced evaluation of the two sides of the argument.

In the use of research such as this, you should keep in mind the following points:

● Make sure you distinguish between fact and opinion. Do not state as a fact what is actually only one viewpoint, e.g., 'Animals suffer dreadfully during scientific experiments'. Show your awareness that this is only one side of the argument with the use of phrases such as 'some people believe' or 'others fear that'.

● Note the stance taken in each source and consider whether it may be biased in some way.

● Do not include too many facts and figures as this will make your essay rather indigestible — you should *interpret* statistics rather than merely quote them.

● Plan your essay carefully.

● **Linkage** will be the key to presenting your argument logically and clearly. Your essay should contain frequent expressions showing how different parts of the argument relate to each other. Look back at pages 35–36 for advice on linkage.

Source (i) Table published by Biomedical Research Education Trust 1996

MAJOR MEDICAL ADVANCES WHICH DEPENDED ON ANIMAL RESEARCH

1900s   Corneal transplants

1920s   Insulin for diabetes

1930s   Modern anaesthetics for surgery
       Diphtheria vaccine

1940s   Antibiotics for infections
       Whooping cough vaccine
       Heart-lung machine for open-heart surgery

1950s   Kidney transplants
       Cardiac pacemakers and replacement heart valves
       Polio vaccine
       Drugs for high blood pressure
       Development of new materials and surgical techniques for joint replacements
       Drugs to treat mental illness

1960s   Rubella vaccine
       Coronary bypass operations
       Heart transplants

1970s   Drugs to treat ulcers
       Drugs to treat asthma
       Drugs to treat leukaemia

1980s   Life-support systems for premature babies
       Drugs to treat viral disease

1990s   Genetic therapy for cystic fibrosis
       Electronic implants for treatment of deafness and paralysis

Source (ii): Extract from BUAV (British Union for the Abolition of Vivisection) pamphlet

What is Vivisection?

"Vivisection" literally means "the cutting up of living animals". But the term is now used generally to describe a variety of experiments which are carried out on over three million animals each year.

Toxicity tests are routinely performed on dogs, rabbits, rats and mice by commercial companies.

Animals are given often huge doses of substances by injection or force feeding and then observed for symptoms such as convulsions, vomiting, breathing difficulties and cries of pain.

Why is Vivisection Wrong?

The BUAV was founded on the philosophy that inflicting pain, suffering and death on helpless animals during experiments is morally wrong. And for many the moral argument is sufficient reason to oppose vivisection. But there is also a wealth of evidence to show that animal experiments are misleading and divert attention and resources away from more fruitful avenues of research.

The notion that results from animal tests can be directly applied to humans has been proved false time and time again.

1. Aspirin causes birth defects in cats but not in humans.
2. Penicillin is toxic to guinea pigs and hamsters.
3. Morphine sedates people but excites cats.
4. Benzene causes leukaemia in humans but not in mice.
5. Saccharin causes cancer in rats but not in humans.

There is always a real danger that, because of our reliance on animal tests, unsafe drugs and other products can be released into the market-place for human use. An example of this was the heart drug Eraldin. Although the drug was thoroughly tested on animals, it had devastating side effects on human patients — including blindness and even death — before it was withdrawn from the market.

Source (iii): Two extracts from a magazine article

(a) When NAVS (National Anti-Vivisection Society) and its sister organisation BUAV began in the late 19th century, their supporters were dismissed as eccentric do-gooders. Today they command impressive support; NAVS, the BUAV and the youth-orientated Animal Aid have a combined membership of around 50,000. These organisations concentrate on public education to win support for their cause but others have employed terror tactics (it was believed that animal rights extremists were responsible for a car bomb — supposedly intended for a research scientist — which seriously injured a small boy in 1990).

(b)

28 year old Andrew Blake suffers from Friedriech's ataxia, a progressive disease of the nervous system. He's confined to a wheelchair, in constant pain and suffers the psychological anguish of steadily losing control of his body. Andrew's consultant believes that a cure for his condition will be found within the next ten years, but the research involves laboratory animals. Andrew has visited the research centre and concedes that some of the animal experiments involve pain and suffering. "But", he argues, "it's difficult to see how research on a painful disease could be done in any other way." For Andrew, the only thing that makes life worth living is the hope of a major breakthrough in medical research. He worries that the climate of opinion against animal research may delay any breakthroughs. "We are the ones," he says, "who pay the price with our extended suffering."

Source (iv): Two personal statements

(a) Statement by Michael B, a scientist engaged in research involving animals.

Through my research, I hope to fight disease and lessen human suffering. Yes, I do put human benefits before animals. Animal rights campaigners often forget that spin-offs from human research have led to enormous benefits for the health of pets and farm animals.

Drug companies are investing heavily in alternatives to animal testing, so the number of animals we use has been going down for years. I do in-vitro experiments for most of my research, which involves growing tissue cultures in test tubes. We also use computers to store and analyse research and cut down on animal tests.

Most of the tests are done without the animals being under anaesthetic, but they aren't very painful — we just give one simple injection or one dose of a drug. The experiments just wouldn't be worth doing if the animal was in pain, because it would be moving around wildly to escape and its nervous and hormonal systems would be going haywire. Those conditions wouldn't produce valid results.

We use a lot of rats for our tests, which have a faster metabolism than humans. That's a problem and we're aware of it, but we use results as a guide to human reactions. Drugs do go through volunteer human testing, but we aim to eliminate many safety risks beforehand.

It's true scientists have made some tragic mistakes. With the appalling thalidomide disaster, the mistake was in not testing the drug on pregnant animals. The Opren story has had bad publicity lately. All drugs have side-effects, and the stronger the dose, the greater the unwanted side effects. Although Opren has been a disaster for many people it has saved others from being bed-ridden with arthritis.

Some people say there are too many similar drugs being produced and companies only develop them to make money. Well, drug companies exist to make a profit. But a lot of drugs which seem identical are subtly different and patients may have to try several before finding the right one.

(b)   Statement from Lesley, a student and animal rights campaigner.

Animal experiments are cruel and a waste of time. They don't prove anything. The way a rat's or rabbit's body works isn't like ours. For example, in the early 1960s, pregnant women took a drug called Thalidomide, which had been tested on animals and "proven" to have no side-effects. But it caused abnormalities in the foetuses and 10,000 babies were born with deformed limbs.

A more recent example is Opren, the anti-arthritis drug. Again, it was tested on animals and considered safe, yet when humans took it there were serious problems. Seventy people died after taking Opren and many thousands suffered damage to skin, eyes, blood circulation, liver and kidneys.

My point is that the tests can't be scientifically justified. Experiments on animals supposedly proved Thalidomide and Opren safe. They weren't, so what was the point of doing the tests? There are other methods of research. Observing humans who actually have the diseases is useful. That's how it was found that smoking causes cancer.

When a drug is being tested, after they've done the animal experiments, the final tests are always on human volunteers. If a drug can't be declared safe until it's been tried on humans, what's the point of testing it on animals at all?

The World Health Organisation has said that only 200 medicines and vaccines are needed to cure known diseases in the UK. Yet there are nearly 20,000 drugs available today. Why? Because drug companies are working in an industry geared to making big profits. We're flooded with drugs we don't need and animals have died for nothing.

Cosmetics testing on animals ended yesterday after the companies licensed by the Government to carry out the processes agreed to a self-imposed ban. Animal rights campaigners hailed it as a landmark in their long-running crusade to end all animal experiments.

However, Home Office minister Lord Williams conceded that the ban would not be wide-ranging enough to stop most tests on animals. About 2·7 million animals are used in medical and scientific research each year in Britain — but only one in 1,000 are cosmetic tests. Last year, 250 rats, guinea pigs and rabbits were killed in "finished product" tests for adverse reactions such as skin sensitivity and eye irritation. More than 2,400 animals were used in tests for new ingredients in cosmetics and toiletries.

But the Government will not be able to stop companies importing cosmetics that have been tested on animals, or even from using overseas laboratories to carry out the tests. Also, some ingredients used in cosmetic products, such as sun screens and preservatives, will be exempt from the ban as they are also used in medical products.

Dr Robert Smith, an expert on alternative test methods, based at Glasgow University, welcomed the ban. He said it was unlikely humans would be used as "guinea-pigs" in future tests because many other methods, such as using corneas from slaughter-houses to test eye irritants, had been developed by the cosmetics industry.

"At the moment, the methodology is improving year by year . . . but because animals and humans are such complex organisms it is only realistic to believe that animals will need to be used for many years to come."

WRITING IN A PARTICULAR GENRE

Genre 4: Prose Fiction

This type of writing is usually a popular choice. You may choose:

a complete **short story**
a **chapter of a novel**
a purely **descriptive** piece of fiction, perhaps aiming at capturing a mood, or painting a picture in words

Recipe for prose fiction

Construct a **plot** line.
Devise one or two **characters**.
Think of a **setting** in which to place your action and characters.
Choose a **theme** and plan what **structure** your story will have.
Finally, make some decisions on the **style** and **expression** you will use.

GETTING STARTED

Before you begin writing, you will find it helpful to analyse the techniques used by professional writers. Remember, you must **not** copy the work of other writers, but it is useful to look at their general approach, and adapt it to suit your own purposes.

To do the following exercises you will need to apply the same skills which you use in Textual Analysis.

In each of the following examples, all from the openings of novels, the author introduces two characters, a setting, and the seeds of conflict to follow.

EXAMPLE (1)

This extract is from Great Expectations *by Charles Dickens. In the first few lines of the novel, the main character introduces himself briefly. Philip Pirrip, known as Pip, explains that he is an orphan, who is being brought up by his older sister.*

Ours was the marsh country, down by the river, within, as the river wound, twenty miles of the sea. My first most vivid and broad impression of the identity of things, seems to me to have been gained on a memorable raw afternoon towards evening. At such a time I found out for certain, that this bleak place overgrown with nettles was the churchyard; and that Philip Pirrip, late of
5   this parish, and also Georgiana, wife of the above, were dead and buried; and that Alexander, Bartholomew, Abraham, Tobias, and Roger, infant children of the aforesaid, were also dead and buried; and that the dark flat wilderness beyond the churchyard, intersected with dykes and mounds and gates, with scattered cattle feeding on it, was the marshes; and that the low leaden line beyond was the river; and that the distant savage lair from which the wind was rushing, was
10 the sea; and that the small bundle of shivers growing afraid of it all and beginning to cry, was Pip.

"Hold your noise!" cried a terrible voice, as a man started up from among the graves at the side of the church porch. "Keep still, you little devil, or I'll cut your throat!"

A fearful man, all in coarse grey, with a great iron on his leg. A man with no hat, and with broken
15 shoes, and with an old rag tied round his head. A man who had been soaked in water, and smothered in mud, and lamed by stones, and cut by flints, and stung by nettles, and torn by briars; who limped and shivered, and glared and growled; and whose teeth chattered in his head as he seized me by the chin.

"O! Don't cut my throat, sir," I pleaded in terror.

(a)   There are two settings here: the wider landscape of the marshes and the smaller area of the graveyard.

Pick out three expressions which describe the setting. What type of mood and atmosphere is established?

(b) What time of day is it, and what is the weather like? What do these features add to the mood?

(c) A second character is introduced in the second and third paragraphs: he will be central to the plot, but here he is anonymous: "a man". Pick out **four** words or phrases which describe the man. Explain how they build up an impression of the character. What **two** contrasting aspects are revealed?

(d) What impression is created of Pip, the narrator?

(e) What plot developments might you expect to follow?

EXAMPLE (2)

This extract is the opening of Consider the Lilies, *by Iain Crichton Smith, a novel set at the time of the Highland Clearances.*

Her name was Mrs Scott and she was an old woman of about seventy. She was sitting on an old chair in front of her cottage when she saw the rider. The rider was Patrick Sellar, factor to the Duke of Sutherland, and he wasn't riding his horse very well, though he felt that in his position he ought to have a horse. He was an ex-lawyer, and horses aren't used to that kind of law. Also,
5   it was a white horse which was one of the reasons why the old woman paid such particular attention to it.

She was just an old woman sitting in the sun watching a few hens scrabble in the dust, and she wasn't really thinking of anything. Dreaming perhaps; for as far as an old woman is concerned there is little difference between reality and dream. She might have been dreaming of her youth
10   or of her son in Canada or of her husband who had been a soldier. Or she might have been watching the horse neither dreaming nor thinking, though half-noticing how it sheered its head away from its rider, its nostrils flaring. She was wearing black, and was very frail-looking.

She didn't know much about horses and she didn't know anything about Patrick Sellar. Nor, for that matter, did he know much about her. As far as he was concerned, she was a disposable
15   object. As far as she was concerned, he was a stranger and to be treated with hospitality even though she was old.

© *Iain Crichton Smith*

(a) Pick out **four** pieces of information we are given about Mrs Scott which arouse sympathy in the reader.

(b) Pick out **three** details the author gives about Patrick Sellar in the first two paragraphs and explain how they affect the reader's feelings towards him.

(c) What clues are there to time and place in the details about the setting?

(d) What hints are given in the third paragraph about what is to come in the novel?

EXAMPLE (3)

This extract is from The Girl at the Lion D'Or *by Sebastian Faulks. It is set in the nineteen thirties.*

In those days the station in Janvilliers had an arched glass roof over the southbound platform as if in imitation of the big domes of St Lazare. When it rained, the impact of the water set up a nervy rattle as the glass echoed and shook against the fancy restraint of its iron framework. There was a more modest rumble emitted by the covered footbridge, while from the gutters
5 there came an awful martyred gurgling as they sought out broken panes and unmended masonry down which to spit the water that was choking them. The thin sound of the locomotive's wheeze as it braced itself for its final three stops up the coast was thus barely audible to the two people who alighted from the train that damp but not untypical Monday night.

One was the driver, who was following the custom of years by climbing down from his cab, hat
10 pulled over his ears, and racing to the side-door of the station buffet where his glass of brandy would be waiting for him. There was no time for conversation — just a quick gulp and he was gone, as usual, scuttling back up the platform, hoisting himself aboard with a word to the fireman and a reinvigorated haul on the levers as the engine hissed and the train set off to arrive, as usual, a minute and a half late at its next stop.

15 The other was a slight, dark-haired girl with two heavy suitcases, frowning into the rain and trying not to feel frightened. She stood in the doorway of the ticket hall, hoping someone would have been sent to fetch her. "Be brave, little Anne, be brave," old Louvet, her guardian, would have said to her if he had been sober, or there, or — for all Anne knew — alive. After a time she did see the long bending approach of headlights, but the car circled the fountains in the middle
20 of the square and disappeared in a spray of water.

© *Sebastian Faulks*

(a) Pick out phrases used by the author in the first paragraph to create an atmosphere of gloom. Referring to at least **two** examples, show how the author uses imagery effectively.

(b) Look at the description of the engine-driver in the second paragraph. What details convey that he is busy, confident and in familiar territory?

(c) How does the character of Anne contrast with him? What details convey she is unsure and in unfamiliar territory? What other details arouse sympathy for Anne?

(d) What features in this scenario intrigue the reader? Suggest what might happen next to Anne.

CONSTRUCTING YOUR STORY

You must now consider the various elements which will be required to construct a story of your own. You may already have some ideas, if your story has been inspired by something you have seen, read or discussed.

PLOT LINES

It has been said that there are only about half a dozen basic plots in all literature.

- "Cinderella": or rags to riches.
- "Romeo and Juliet" or boy meets girl / boy loses girl.
- "David and Goliath" or winning against the odds.
- "Spider and Fly" or an innocent falling into a trap.
- "Nemesis" or fate catching up with a wrong-doer.
- "Virtue rewarded".

There may be variations. For example, the "Cinderella" figure could be male; the story could go back to rags again. *The Verger* by Somerset Maugham is an example of a variant on "Cinderella", although the Cinderella figure is an elderly man rather than a young girl.

The Landlady by Roald Dahl would be an example of "Spider and Fly". Think of some well-known stories and consider what pattern they follow. Can you think of any other basic plot lines to add to the six given above?

There are even simpler patterns, such as a chase, a quest or a race against time.

THEMES

You could also approach your story by choosing a theme. Common themes include love, money, power, revenge, survival, justice, betrayal.

Can you think of other themes to add to this list?

SETTING

You must choose where and when your story will take place. Creating a convincing setting requires careful descriptive writing which enables the reader to picture a scene and also evokes a mood. You might consider trying to re-create a past age. Another idea which has proved popular is to use a real place as your setting: you can describe a location which you actually know well and set fictitious characters and events within it.

FOR PRACTICE

- Think of a place you know well. Choose one or two locations within the place which you think might provide a suitable backdrop for a story. Write two or three paragraphs of description, including some names of real buildings, shops, streets, etc.

- Write two paragraphs of description of a wholly fictitious location. For example, you might choose a grim dockland street, a stretch of wild rocky coast, a stately home, or a fishing harbour.

If you find you are successful in doing this, you might consider expanding your writing into a wholly descriptive piece in which creating a mood and atmosphere is the main purpose.

CHARACTERS

If you aim to write a short story or to write the opening chapter of a novel, you will need to introduce at least one character.

It will be important to bring your character to life with a few well chosen pieces of description. Look at the following extracts which are examples of excellent character drawing.

The first is from a novel, *The Go-Between*, by L.P. Hartley, and describes the moment the narrator sees his friend's beautiful sister, Marion, for the first time. The second is from a short story, *The Doll's House*, by Katherine Mansfield.

Extract 1

> Her father's long eyelids drooped over her eyes, leaving under them a glint of blue so deep and liquid that it might have been shining through an unshed tear. Her hair was bright with sunshine, but her face, which was full like her mother's, only pale rose-pink instead of cream, wore a stern brooding look that her small curved nose made almost hawk-like. She looked formidable then, almost as formidable as her mother. A moment later she opened her eyes — I remember the sudden burst of blue — and her face lit up. So that is what it is to be beautiful, I thought.

Extract 2

> Our Else wore a long white dress, rather like a nightgown, and a pair of little boy's boots. But whatever our Else wore she would have looked strange. She was a tiny wishbone of a child, with cropped hair and enormous solemn eyes — a little white owl. Nobody had ever seen her smile; she scarcely ever spoke.

Extract 1

(a)   L.P. Hartley's description of Marion is an intriguing combination of appealing and unappealing features. Pick out three expressions which make her sound attractive and three which are unattractive.

(b)   What feelings do you think the narrator has towards Marion?

(c)   What does this extract lead you to expect Marion to be like as a character?

Extract 2

(d)   What impression does Katherine Mansfield's character "our Else" make on you? Do you see her as pathetic? Comical? Vulnerable? Peculiar? Disturbing?

Pick out one or two expressions and explain your response.

> **FOR PRACTICE**

Make notes for a fictional character. Before you describe the character physically, you should decide a little about his / her personality and background, and what impression you intend to make on the reader. Describe your character in around five–ten sentences.

Remember, the test of a well-drawn character is that the reader should wish to know more about him or her. What motivates the character will direct the plot and your depiction of this motivation is what will engage the reader and make the plot engrossing. It is very important that you feel you "know" your characters before you begin writing about what they do.

FORM AND STRUCTURE

Prose fiction may take the form of a **short story** or an **episode from a novel**.

A short story must be complete: generally, it requires a beginning, a middle and an end. You must establish one or more characters, create a situation which is then developed and finally brought to a conclusion. Obviously it is necessary that the situation be simple enough so that this is possible to do in a satisfactory way within the word limit.

The simplest structure is the **linear** one, where events succeed one another in order of time. You might, however, choose a **flashback** pattern. Here, the story begins by showing the outcome, then flashes back to the beginning and continues in a full circle to arrive where the story started, showing how and why events turned out as they did. Alternatively, you can have a more complex **dual** structure where the present and past alternate. A good example of this is Alice Walker's story *Roselily*, in which the opening words of the marriage service form a framework for the flashbacks which fill in the story.

> Dearly Beloved
>
> She dreams; dragging herself across the world. A small girl in her mother's white robe and veil, knee raised waist high through a bowl of quicksand soup. The man who stands beside her is against this standing on the front porch of her house, being married to the sound of cars whizzing by on highway 61.

Yet another **structure** is an alternation between two characters. In Bernard McLaverty's *Father and Son*, which has as its theme the communication gap between a father and his son who has become involved with the IRA, McLaverty switches between the son's and father's point of view.

> I do not sleep. My father does not sleep. The sound of ambulances criss-crosses the dark. I sleep with the daylight. It is safe. At night I hear his bare feet click as he lifts them, walking the lino. The front door shudders as he leaves.
>
> My son is breaking my heart. It is already broken. Is it my fault there is no woman in the house? Is it my fault a good woman should die?

Writing a chapter of a novel offers different opportunities. The opening chapter is the obvious choice. Since you do not need to resolve the action, you can develop your characters and setting in some depth, and offer only the initial stages of the plot. You must end with some degree of a "cliff-hanger" to leave the reader wanting more. Make it clear that this *is* intended as an opening chapter, otherwise you risk the danger of having your work misjudged as a complete story.

EXPRESSION

You must decide whether to present the story in the **first** or **third person**. You might try the ambitious technique of alternating between first and third person narratives: but this must be deliberate — a not uncommon but very damaging error is for this change to occur accidentally!

You may wish to use **dialogue** in your story. This must always be treated carefully: you should cut any dialogue which is not contributing meaningfully in some way. Unnecessary dialogue slows up the narrative and can confuse the reader.

You are strongly encouraged to make use of **dialect** such as Scots language. This can give a very strong sense of place and add authenticity. Use what you know: if your local area has a distinctive dialect, try to capture precisely its particular sounds and features of grammar and vocabulary.

Colloquial language or any non-standard English may be used but with the stipulation that any departure from the norm "to achieve particular effects" must clearly be intentional. If, for example, you make a character speak ungrammatically, it must be evident from the good structure of the rest of your narrative that you have planned this consciously.

Imagery and **symbolism**. It is worth while making an effort to include techniques like these. Symbolism has been mentioned in the discussion of the short story, *The Bike*. A famous example is to be found in Thomas Hardy's novel, *Tess of the D'Urbervilles*. Tess has just murdered her husband in the upper room of a boarding house before running off to join her lover. The landlady is in the room beneath when the blood starts to ooze through her ceiling:

> In reflecting she leant back in her chair. As she did so her eyes glanced casually over the ceiling till they were arrested by a spot in the middle of its white surface which she had never noticed there before. It was about the size of a wafer when she first observed it, but it speedily grew as large as the palm of her hand, and then she could perceive that it was red. The oblong white ceiling, with this scarlet blot in the midst, had the appearance of a gigantic ace of hearts.

Here the bloodstain in the shape of the ace of hearts is symbolic as it is the result of a crime of passion.

THE ENDING

The six plots mentioned on page 78 have conventional endings. For example, Cinderella goes from rags to riches, and David overcomes Goliath. It is important to have a strong ending, as that is what will make your final impression. It is worth while taking particular care over expression.

Possibilities include a happy ending, in which all loose ends are tied up, or a sad ending in which a character is disappointed or suffers in some way. There may be a "twist" of some kind. A "twist" is a surprise ending, but it should be logical: there should be hidden clues so that the reader does not feel cheated. Sometimes, the ending may be left deliberately ambiguous. In Roald Dahl's *The Landlady*, which was mentioned as an example of the "Spider and Fly" plot, the main character is left at the end with someone whom he suspects of being a serial killer: we don't know if he escapes or not.

FOR PRACTICE

Make a list of short stories you have read recently. Try to remember the ending and decide if you did or did not like it.

PLANNING YOUR STORY

You should now be ready to draft out some ideas for plot, theme, setting and character. At this stage you should also sketch out some alternatives. For example if you decide on a "boy meets girl" scenario, you might think of alternative "happy" and "unhappy" outcomes. Look at the general hints on planning on pages 47 and 48.

WRITING YOUR STORY

Having sketched out a plan, you should now attempt the first draft of your story. Look at the advice on pages 48 and 49 concerning redrafting and presentation.

Genre 5 : Poem, or set of thematically linked poems

Whole books have been devoted to poetry writing and if you intend to try this option, you would be best to consult one of these specialist publications. However, a few words of advice and caution will be included here, as well as a short exercise in textual analysis.

APPROACHES

One approach to a poem is to write a piece of prose first which is descriptive or reflective. You can then experiment with your ideas and language, transposing them into poetic form. Alternatively, you might begin by writing down a list of random thoughts and ideas, and then try arranging them.

WHAT CHOICES MUST BE MADE

(a) **Topics:** Firstly, exactly the same advice for choosing a topic applies to poetry as to creative prose writing. Reading a piece of literature, hearing a piece of music, seeing a painting, viewing a landscape or a simple observation from daily life — any experience may act as a trigger for your imagination.

Generally, if you wish a poem to have impact, you are best to choose a narrow area rather than a wide one; or a personal experience rather than a vaguer, wider issue. For example, the general topic of "Homelessness" is *less* likely to be successful than an observation of one particular homeless person. The progression of ideas might lead on to a wider issue, but you must try to find something original to say: this can be quite a challenge if the topic is a popular one.

(b) **Forms:** You might try a particular form like a sonnet, which will require very careful crafting to get the rhyme and metre correct. It is more likely you will try some form of free verse. However, it is important that you do not regard this as merely an easier option. You should consider sound very carefully, and techniques such as alliteration and assonance; stress and rhythm.

(c)   **Expression:** Poetry demands a highly concentrated form of language, in which the meaning and sound of every word is significant. You will gain credit from intelligent use of imagery and symbolism. Writing in Scots is an option to be encouraged for those who know a particular dialect well.

LENGTH

The stipulation is that the length of a poem "depends on the chosen form". Obviously, if you have chosen a sonnet, it would be 14 lines long. However, you must be careful of a poetry option appearing too thin. The suggestion of a set of thematically linked poems might be a guard against this, although quality is certainly more important than quantity!

It is very likely that you will require to do a great deal of drafting and redrafting. It is interesting to look at the manuscripts of well-known poets and to look at the editing they have done before producing the finished poems.

FOR PRACTICE

To give an idea of the kind of redrafting you should do of your own poems, consider the example below. On the right is printed a very well known sonnet by the 1st World War poet Wilfred Owen (1893–1918). On the left is an earlier draft of the same poem. Answering the questions should help illustrate how editing and redrafting made his finished poem more effective. A marking scheme is attached so that this exercise may be done as an individual textual analysis. It may also be done orally in pairs or groups.

	Anthem to Dead Youth		**Anthem for Doomed Youth**
	What passing bells for you who die in herds?		What passing bells for those who die as cattle?
	— Only the monstrous anger of more guns,		— Only the monstrous anger of the guns,
	— Only the stuttering rifle's rattled words		— Only the stuttering rifle's rapid rattle
	Can patter out your hasty orisons.		Can patter out their hasty orisons.
	No chants for you, nor balms, nor wreaths, nor bells,	5	No mockeries now for them, no prayers, nor bells,
	— Nor any voice of mourning, save the choirs,		— Nor any voice of mourning, save the choirs,
	The shrill demented choirs of wailing shells;		The shrill demented choirs of wailing shells;
	— And bugles calling for you from sad shires.		— And bugles calling for them from sad shires.
	What candles may we hold to speed you all?		What candles may be held to speed them all?
	Not in the hands of boys, but in their eyes	10	Not in the hands of boys, but in their eyes
	Shall shine the holy lights of long goodbyes.		Shall shine the holy glimmers of goodbyes.
	The pallor of girls' brows shall be your pall,		The pallor of girls' brows shall be their pall,
	Your flowers the tenderness of mortal minds;		Their flowers the tenderness of patient minds;
	And each slow dusk a drawing-down of blinds.		And each slow dusk a drawing-down of blinds.

(a) Look at the change in line 1 from "in herds" to "as cattle". What does the phrase "as cattle" add to the sense of
    (i)   the vulnerability of the victims of war;
    (ii) the degree of dignity of their deaths;
    (iii) the quantity and mechanical nature of their deaths?   **6**

(b) Try reading the two versions of line 2 aloud. The change from "more guns" to "the guns" alters the rhythm as "the" is unstressed.
    (i)   How does this affect the amount of emphasis on the word "guns"?
    (ii) Which sound is more dominant in each version, "m" or "g"?   **2**

(c) In line 3, how does the change from "rattled words" to "rapid rattle" affect the sound of the line?   **1**

(d) How does Owen change the tone with his choice of the word "mockeries" in line 5 to replace some of the religious words used in the earlier version?   **1**

(e) Can you suggest how the poet's alteration to line 11 in the second version affects both sense and sound?   **2**

(f) Owen altered the word "dead" in the title to "doomed".
    (i)   How does this enlarge the scope of the poem?   **2**
    (ii) What does the sound of the word "doomed" contribute?   **1**

(g) The most wide-ranging change is the alteration from second person to third person. Instead of addressing the dead, Owen talks of them. How does this affect the tone of the poem?   **2**

(h) Comment on any four of the changes. Say why you do or do not think the edited version is an improvement on the original.   **8**

                                                                    Total 25

WRITING IN A PARTICULAR GENRE

Genre 6 : Dramatic Script (for example, scene, monologue, sketch)

As in the case of prose, you have the option of attempting a complete piece of drama in the form of a one-act play or sketch, or presenting a single scene intended to form part of a longer play. A one-act play is similar to a short story in that it will have a complete plot line, with a beginning, middle and end. The term "sketch" is generally applied to a slighter piece: possibly a piece of comedy or a dialogue between two people, perhaps illustrating a particular theme. A monologue is a narrative piece to be delivered by one person. A radio play has certain advantages as you do not need to consider the visual aspects which are necessary for the stage or television.

You should follow the same steps as you would for prose fiction, in selecting a plot or theme, characters, a setting, an outcome, and a structure. Of course, your topic need not be fiction: you might choose to dramatise a real event. Events such as the Gunpowder Plot, or the discovery of Tutankhamen's tomb, are by their very nature dramatic. A piece of literature is very likely to provide you with a context for drama. The playwright Tom Stoppard had a great success with *Rosencrantz and Guildenstern are Dead*, in which he imagined the off-stage happenings in Shakespeare's *Hamlet*, and made two of Shakespeare's minor characters into major ones. You might try the same thing with another of Shakespeare's plays: for example you could dramatise the courtship of Theseus and Hippolyta as a prequel to *A Midsummer Night's Dream*.

Planning will be very important. Many playwrights begin by sketching out a play in the form of a prose narrative, before putting it into dramatic form: you might find this helpful.

Choosing drama as a genre will require some extra planning. You will have to consider how your characters will be placed on the stage, their movements and their gestures. You may wish to give details regarding the set.

PRESENTATION AND LAYOUT

It is unlikely that you will be attempting this option if you are unfamiliar with the layout of a dramatic text. You will need a title and a list of characters at the beginning. Inverted commas are not used for dialogue, but each speech must begin on a new line following the name of the character. Stage directions should be placed in square brackets, and, if printed, printed in italics.

Some writers, such as Bernard Shaw and Tennessee Williams, give very detailed stage directions which give guidance to actors and directors. In the middle of *Cat on a Hot Tin Roof*, for example, Tennessee Williams explains how he is "trying to capture the true experience in a group of people". The following extract from Shaw's *Pygmalion* shows many of the conventions of script writing.

This is part of the famous scene where Eliza Doolittle, the Cockney flower girl, is being presented in society for the first time by Professor Higgins, who is trying to win a bet that he can pass her off as an upper class lady.

Characters' names in capitals

LIZA. [*Now quite at her ease*] You see, it's like this. If a man has a bit of a conscience it always takes him when he's sober; and then it makes him low-spirited. A drop of booze just takes that off and makes him happy. [*To Freddy, who is in convulsions of suppressed laughter*] Here! What are you sniggering at?

Stage directions in brackets, in italics.

FREDDY. The new small talk. You do it so awfully well.

A new line is taken for each new speaker.

LIZA. If I was doing it proper, what was you laughing at? [*To Higgins*]
Have I said anything I oughtn't?

MRS HIGGINS. [*Interposing*] Not at all, Miss Doolittle.

LIZA. Well, that's a mercy, anyhow. [*Expansively*] What I always say is —

Inverted commas are **not** used to mark characters' words.

HIGGINS. [*rising and looking at his watch*] Ahem!

LIZA. [*looking round at him; taking the hint; and rising*] Well: I must go. [*They all rise. Freddy goes to the door*] So pleased to have met you. Goodbye. [*She shakes hands with Mrs Higgins*].

MRS HIGGINS. Goodbye.

LIZA. Goodbye, Colonel Pickering.

PICKERING. Goodbye, Miss Doolittle. [*They shake hands*].

LIZA. [*nodding to the others*] Goodbye all.

FREDDY. [*opening the door for her*] Are you walking across the Park, Miss Doolittle? If so —

Stage directions may interrupt the dialogue, which would be continuous on stage.

LIZA. [*with perfectly elegant diction*] Walk! Not bloody likely. [*Sensation*] I am going in a taxi. [*She goes out*].

EXPRESSION

Since you are working within the medium of spoken English, you are likely to choose a colloquial register for the dialogue. However, it should be clear that any departure from Standard English is deliberate. Punctuation, for example, will be very important. It is also advisable to be cautious in the use of any language which might cause offence.

Dialect forms such as Scots can be very effective in drama. Tony Roper's play *The Steamie*, which presented a slice of life in a Glasgow wash-house, has been very popular. You might try offering a similar view of a community with a different setting. The dramatic monologues of Liz Lochhead would be good models to follow, as they are excellent examples of vivid character portrayal. They show an accurate ear for the speech patterns of Glasgow, in addition to being both entertaining and thought-provoking. Presenting the authentic voice of your local area is likely to be an attainable and successful goal.

FINDING A CONTEXT

You now have a clearer idea of what the different genres of writing involve. Now all you have to do is write the essay!

It is difficult to decide on a topic when you have complete freedom of choice. However, it is likely, and desirable, that your writing will arise from a context. This simply means that something you have read, seen or discussed will trigger off an idea for writing something of your own. You will still have a number of choices to make which will be explored in the following pages, but it is easier if you have some kind of stimulus which sets you thinking in a particular direction.

In the critical essay section of this book we have looked at Shakespeare's *Macbeth* in some detail. *Macbeth* will also provide an example of how one literary text may provide stimuli for various kinds of writing.

Group A: Expressive

1   *Reflective / personal*

- Write your reflections on a visit to the play in the theatre, or on your experiences in taking some part in a production of the play.

- Write a reflective essay on one of the themes of the play: jealousy; ambition; the effects of power; the qualities required by a king or leader; the balance of fate and character in determining the course of life, the existence of evil.

2   *Persuasive*

- Write an essay putting forward a convincing case that Shakespeare's plays are still relevant to a modern audience / readership. (You could also argue for the converse!)

3   *Argumentative*

- Write a balanced discussion on the pros and cons of studying film versions of a play rather than reading the text only.

- At the time of the play of *Macbeth*, Scotland was an independent country. Write an essay on the advantages and disadvantages to Scotland if full independence were restored.

Group B: **Creative**

4   *Prose Fiction:*

- Write a story involving two friends who become rivals.

- Write a story in which someone is persuaded into doing something they regret.

- Write a ghost story set at "Birnam Wood" and "Dunsinane".

- Many quotations from the play have been used as titles, e.g., "The Blanket of the Dark"; "Instruments of Darkness". Choose one of these or another evocative quotation of your own choice and write an imaginative composition.

5   *Poem or set of thematically linked poems*

- Compose a set of poems with linking themes of happiness; hope; despair.

- Write a poem describing a ruined castle which has seen scenes of great conflict and bloodshed in the past.

6   *A Dramatic Script*

- Compose a scene in which one character persuades another into wrong-doing.

- Compose a scene involving Banquo and Fleance, presenting events from their point of view. (It would be quite acceptable to put the dialogue in modern English.)

The short story *The Bike*, which you also looked at earlier, could provide similar contexts for creative writing :

Group A: **Expressive**

1   *Reflective / personal*

- Write a personal essay reflecting on either:
  (i) buying a much longed for item
  (ii) a broken relationship
  (iii) early work experiences.

- (More difficult) Annie's experiences may help the reader of the story to cope with similar disappointments in their own lives. Write a discussion of one or two episodes of fiction or experiences of fictional characters which you feel have influenced the way you see yourself and the world in general.

2 / 3 *Persuasive / Argumentative*

- "Teaching young people about life is more effectively done through the study of literature than directly through PSE lessons."

  Write an essay either putting forward this point of view, or its contrary, or write a balanced discussion of the topic.

Group B: **Creative**

4   *Prose Fiction*

- Write a story centred round an object. You might choose: a watch; a piece of jewellery; a piece of clothing; a photograph; a picture.
  (You might aim at the object's assuming a symbolic significance, in the same way that Annie's bike, progressing from new to a wreck, represents her relationship.)

Selecting a topic for a piece of writing from within a context should enable you to approach it with a degree of authority from having explored an issue in some depth.

For example, if you choose the topic "Friends who become rivals", you will have studied a similar progression in the relationship of Macbeth and Banquo, and analysed the reasons for the deterioration of their friendship. You may then invent another situation in which a relationship changes, but for different reasons. For the ghost story, scenes from the play might have even more direct relevance.

SELECT YOUR OWN TOPIC

Choose a piece of literature you have enjoyed. In groups, think of possible "spin-off" topics for writing in the categories listed.

You should now choose one or two topics which appeal to you. Then look at the advice given in the relevant sections on the type of writing you are attempting.

Checklist for Writing

✔ Your writing will be judged on the criteria of **content**, **structure**, **expression** and **technical accuracy**.

✔ Keep a **plan** and early **drafts** of your writing piece.

✔ The types of writing you may choose are: Reflective / Personal; Persuasive; Argumentative; Prose Fiction; Poetry; Drama.

✔ Beware of **plagiarism**.

PART THREE

Writing The Personal Study

Writing The Personal Study

"A man ought to read just as inclination leads him, for what he reads as a task will do him little good."
(Dr Samuel Johnson, 1709–1784)

WHAT YOU WILL BE ASKED TO DO

Perhaps some of the work you have to do in English makes you agree with Dr Johnson's comment. However, if you are undertaking a Personal Study in Literature, the outcome of this part of the course will be a review of a text of your own choice.

In most cases the text will be a novel. However, you might also choose a play, a selection of poems, or a comparison of two or more of these. There are other options, too — biography, journalism or a non-print topic, such as a film. Your teacher or tutor will be able to give you further details on these options.

This section concentrates on giving advice on writing your review. Many of the skills explained in *Part One: Writing a Critical Essay* are relevant here.

- The review should contain your own ideas.
- The text(s) will not be taught in class (although, of course, you can and should seek your teacher's advice).
- You choose your own topic rather than being given a set question.
- Your review should have a clear and relevant line of thought.
- You should concentrate on a particular aspect of the text rather than trying to write a general review.
- You should discuss style as well as the content of the text.

One of the stipulations of the Personal Study is that you must choose your own text, although your teacher or tutor may provide guidance. So how do you go about making the right selection?

What you should avoid

✗   You must **not** choose a text which you have previously been taught in class.

✗   You should **not** choose abridged or simplified texts. (Although you may choose a text translated from another language.)

✗   There are some things which are best avoided, or at least used with caution. *Genre fiction*, such as detective, romantic or horror novels, however entertaining, rarely yields good reviews. This would include the work of such authors as James Herbert, Stephen King, Danielle Steele and John Grisham. Caution should also be exercised in the choice of books containing material or language which might be deemed offensive.

What you should consider

✔   *Is the book of recognised literary merit?*
This means that the material will have sufficient depth of content and stylistic artistry to allow you to develop some worthwhile results from your study of it. If you choose an unsuitable text or one of inferior quality you will be handicapping yourself at the outset. There are several texts which are very commonly taught, and which some people regard as suffering from over-exposure. These include Golding's *Lord of the Flies*, Harper Lee's *To Kill a Mocking-Bird*, Steinbeck's *Of Mice and Men* and Salinger's *The Catcher in the Rye*. However, these are excellent pieces of literature with which young people find it easy to engage, and there seems no reason why they should be avoided by readers discovering them for the first time since they are still capable of stimulating candidates to produce good reviews.

✔   *What did you enjoy reading when you were younger?*
Good children's fiction such as that written by L.M. Montgomery, Louisa May Alcott, J.R.R. Tolkein or Alan Garner can prove worthwhile. *The Adventures of Tom Sawyer* by Mark Twain, for example, was originally written for an adult readership, prompting the choice of a topic considering the book's different appeal to adults and children.

✔ *What have you enjoyed reading more recently?*
If you like a particular author, you may wish to look at another of his books. If the theme of a book studied in class interested you, you could consider another work which deals with a similar topic. For example, one candidate became interested in the theme of racial discrimination through her previous reading of *To Kill a Mocking Bird*, and this interest led her to read Alan Paton's *Cry the Beloved Country*, a tragic story of two fathers and their sons set in South Africa during the time of apartheid.

✔ *Do your tastes lie with classic writers of the past?*
Classic writers, such as Charles Dickens, Jane Austen, Thomas Hardy, the Brontës, George Eliot and Henry James almost always make rewarding choices, although you may be better to choose one of their shorter works. Even a relatively short text such as Dickens's *A Christmas Carol* is capable of providing a great variety of responses. If you do make the effort to review a "difficult" text such as Dickens's *Bleak House* or Thackeray's *Vanity Fair,* it is very likely that you will be rewarded with a good mark. Examiners have often noted that candidates engage just as well, if not better, with classic texts.

✔ *Do you like to keep up with current trends?*
As far as modern texts are concerned, you may get ideas from the best-sellers lists which are published in newspapers and magazines. Consider those which have won or been shortlisted for some of the major fiction competitions such as the Booker, Orange or Guardian fiction prizes. Generally, publishers will display this information on the covers of the books. Writers who have been prominent on these lists include Ian McEwan, Beryl Bainbridge, William Trevor, Carol Shields, Roddy Doyle and William McIlvanney. Many bookshops now have excellent displays of material with recommendations and information to help you.

✔ *Have you enjoyed watching a film or TV adaptation?*
A very successful T.V. adaptation of Jane Austen's *Pride and Prejudice* prompted many people to return to the original novel. This can be a very good way of discovering an interesting text — but beware of the "book-of-the-film". These are novels written quickly, based on the screenplay of a successful film or TV show. They are generally of minimal literary merit and are best avoided.

✔ *Have you a particular interest in Scottish writing?*
Scottish texts are a good choice since they are likely to promote close engagement with material which is close to home. A separate lists of Scottish texts is included in the appendix.

✔ *Have you a particular interest in another country, or culture?*
You may choose a text translated from another language. If you have a connection with an ethnic group, a choice of text reflecting this heritage could prove rewarding.

When you read the book for the first time, you should simply be concerned to understand what is happening and to notice some general characteristics about the author's style of writing (e.g., is the book written in the first person?).

After your first reading you may have been able to form a vague idea of a topic that you might like to write about, such as character development or a particular theme. With almost any book of literary merit, you should be left with a feeling that you have learnt something new and worthwhile about life and human nature. As the novelist Anthony Powell once said, "People think that because a novel's invented it isn't true. Exactly the reverse is the case."

You should then go through the book a second time to test whether there is enough material to make your provisional topic a suitable one. If the copy of the book is your own rather than a library or school copy, it is a good idea to mark relevant passages, and then make a list of page references. If, for instance, you are thinking about writing on the development of a character, make a list of all the places in the book which give insights into that character's mind and behaviour. If any ideas occur to you while you are doing this, then write them down.

A popular novel is *The Changeling*, by Robin Jenkins, which tells the story of a well-meaning teacher called Charlie Forbes. One of his pupils, Tom Curdie, lives in a slum and Charlie decides to take Tom on holiday with his own family, with tragic results. The following are notes jotted down by a reader of *The Changeling*:

page 13	*Example of Charlie's idealism*
page 14	*Example of his wife's more realistic outlook on life*
page 14	*Example of conflict between husband and wife*
page 15	*Summary of Tom's rules for survival*
page 15	*Description of the poverty of Tom's surroundings*
page 16	*Use of dialect to reflect social background*

These comments will, of course, be disjointed at this stage. It is when you look back over them that you will begin to see a pattern emerging. For instance, you may notice that you have frequently made notes about the importance of the setting and this might lead you to consider the inter-relationship of plot and setting as a possible topic to write on.

WRITING THE PERSONAL STUDY

Teachers and examiners have observed that the more specific the chosen task, the more productive the outcome tends to be.

Let's imagine you have decided to write on *The Changeling* and you are considering various possible titles for your Personal Study.

Topic one:

A Review of The Changeling

Clearly, this would not be specific enough. Such a title gives no indication of which aspects you are going to cover, and the review would probably be too general: it might not even amount to much more than a retelling of the story.

A better way to arrive at a topic is to think about the book in terms of its plot, characterisation, setting, themes and style. On your first reading, it would be a good idea to make some notes under each of these five categories. At the end you may find you have said a good deal about, say, characterisation and not so much about setting, for instance. This will help to guide you towards choosing a suitable topic to write on.

Topic two:

A study of characterisation in The Changeling

This is certainly better than the first suggested title. However, the way you word your topic should give some clue as to how the essay is going to develop. This title doesn't do that. Nor does it suggest which characters are going to be discussed. To look at every character in the book would be too much, and the danger is that the review would simply end up as a disjointed series of character sketches.

Topic three:

A study of the relationship between Charlie Forbes and Tom Curdie in The Changeling

Again, this is an improvement as it is more specific. The danger remains, however, that the review could still be a narrative of what happens to these two characters from the beginning of the novel to the end.

Topic four:

"A study of why the relationship between Charlie Forbes and Tom Curdie ends in tragedy."

Another improvement, but most students would still tell the story of the relationship rather than explaining why it failed.

Topic five:

> *"A study of the various factors which caused the relationship between Charlie Forbes and Tom Curdie to end in tragedy."*

This rightly places the greatest emphasis on the analysis of why things happened, rather than simply a narrative of what happened.

FOR PRACTICE

In pairs or in groups, discuss how suitable you think these Personal Study titles might be. It will not matter if you haven't read the books referred to; just try to assess how much the suggested title tells you about the content of the review.

1. A study of John Buchan's use of suspense in *The Thirty-Nine Steps*.

2. A study of how John Buchan uses settings to heighten suspense in *The Thirty-Nine Steps*.

3. The relationship between Willy Loman and his son Biff in Arthur Miller's play, *Death of a Salesman*.

4. A study of the problems faced by Willy Loman in *Death of a Salesman*.

5. An analysis of the effects of Willy Loman's self-delusion on himself and other characters in *Death of a Salesman*.

6. An examination of how Arthur Miller's use of various techniques in *Death of a Salesman* helps the audience to understand the problems faced by the main character, Willy Loman.

7. The development of the relationship of Elizabeth Bennet and Mr D'Arcy in *Pride and Prejudice*.

8. An analysis of how far Elizabeth Bennet and Mr D'Arcy represent the "pride" and "prejudice" of the title of Jane Austen's novel.

9. A study of relationships in *Pride and Prejudice*, analysing how Jane Austen exposes the flaws of other couples to provide a foil for the ideal pairing of Elizabeth Bennet and Mr D'Arcy.

10. Jane Austen's presentation of marriage in *Pride and Prejudice*.

EXPANDING YOUR INITIAL IDEAS

● *Creating a line of argument*

Assuming that you have chosen an aspect of the book to write about, you must now express your topic in such a way that it allows for a **developing argument**. The structure of your review will be weak if it is merely a **list** of separate points or a **narrative** of events.

One way of doing this is to divide your argument into separate stages and deal with each of these in turn. This does not mean that your review falls into a number of unconnected sections, or that it follows a dull and mechanical "firstly", "secondly", "thirdly" approach. A developing argument means that stage two of your case builds on and develops stage one, stage three develops out of stage two, and so on. You must include in the opening paragraph a clear indication of your intention: "In this review I intend to . . .".

It can also be helpful for your introductory paragraph to outline the stages of your argument. While it would not be desirable for every review to follow an identical format, you may find it useful to use sentence patterns such as these in your opening paragraph:

> *I will begin by suggesting that . . .*
> > *I will then go on to discuss how . . .*
> > > *and will end by considering . . .*

Other useful words that could be used here are *examine*, *analyse* and *argue*.

● *Linking from one stage to the next*

The use of linking words and phrases like *however*, *furthermore*, *consequently* and so on has already been discussed on page 35. It is helpful to use linking sentences which form a "bridge" from one stage of your argument to the next. For instance:

> *So far, I have shown that . . .*
> *This, however, is not the only factor in explaining . . .*
> *This raises another interesting aspect . . .*

● *Expressing a personal response*

The *generalisation — evidence — comment* approach explained on pages 11–15 should be used throughout your review. However, you should remember that as this part of the course is based on your own choice of text rather than a book taught in class, you should place more emphasis on your personal responses. On the simplest level, this may mean that you use the first person "I" in expressions such as

> *I felt sympathetic to . . . at this point of the story because . . .*
> *The tone of . . . 's comment made me particularly aware of . . .*
> *After thinking it over . . . I was left with the feeling that . . .*

But there is more to personal response than merely using the first person. You must aim in some way to convey that reading your book has genuinely made you think about the issues raised by the story, and that you have become involved with the characters — or even, perhaps, identified with one of them. The following extract illustrates one student's handling of the idea of personal response:

> My study of *The Crucible* showed me that although we may hide our evil, it is always there, and will not rest until we have fully admitted it, either to ourselves or to others. I thought it interesting that Proctor could not have his goodness until he had confessed his evil, however much he appeared to have it before. Hence, my study of this play deepened my understanding of the human capacity for good and evil.

Notice that a personal tone is not the same as an informal, chatty tone. It is perfectly possible to combine a personal approach with a formal, analytical style of expression.

● *Revealing an insight into the writer's use of literary / linguistic technique*

It is not enough to write about the plot, characterisation, and so on; you must also consider the writer's style. To do this you should be able to use critical terminology — in other words, technical terms to do with literature. *

Obviously, no two writers write in exactly the same way. As you read you should try to identify what you think are the most distinctive features of the way your author writes. Ask yourself what makes his style different from another writer you are familiar with.

Whichever book you are reading, some of the following points are bound to be relevant.

---

* For fuller definitions of these terms, see
Language Skills for Higher English by the same authors.

Narrative standpoint:

Does the author use a *persona* (i.e., does he write from the point of view of one of the characters in the book)? If so, what are the implications of this for the novel? What limitations does it impose? What advantages does it have?

Does the author tell the story as an *omniscient narrator* (i.e., can he see into the minds of all the characters in the book)? What advantages does this approach have?

Does the author use more than one *narrative voice*? For instance, the book may alternate between two different narrators, or different literary forms may be employed. Narrative chapters may alternate with letters or diary entries, for example.

Narrative tone:

Does the author express opinions as he writes? If so, why does he do this? What is the effect on the reader? Does it add a particular tone (such as a humour or irony) to the work?

Structure:

Is the story told in a straightforward chronological manner (i.e., a narrative of events in the order in which they happened)? Does the author vary the time sequence — e.g., by using flashbacks? How does this affect the story?

Does the book have a main and a sub-plot — or several sub-plots? How are these introduced separately and how do they begin to weave together?

Can the book be subdivided into sections or groups of chapters? What is the point of these divisions?

Use of language:

Is there any particular style of expression that characterises the book?
> Formal / informal language
> Use of archaic language
> Use of a local dialect

Is the author's style purely factual / narrative or are descriptive passages present? If so, what is the function of these? At what points do they occur?

Is the language used exclusively literal or is the author's style rich in metaphor, simile and other figurative devices?

Are there any particular descriptive motifs running through the book (e.g., metaphors which are used more than once, or details that are frequently referred to)? Are these being used to stand for / symbolise something else?

In general, look for examples of the author's individual word choice which you think are particularly well-chosen and try to explain why these are effective.

Obviously, the list above is not exhaustive, but it will at least help you to start focusing on the stylistic aspects of your book. You are bound to find some of these points in your chosen text — but don't forget the possibility that another technique altogether could be used by your author.

REMEMBER

A poorly written or merely adequate review will concentrate more or less entirely on the **content** of the text.

A more competent review will talk about the **style** of the book as well.

But the best reviews will *combine* the discussion of both **content** and **style**.

If you just tack on a paragraph or two about the author's style at the end of your review, this material is not likely to be properly integrated into your argument. A much better approach is to comment on stylistic arguments throughout the review, as and when the style of the book seems to you particularly relevant to the content.

You may well feel that this is easy enough to say but not so easy to put into practice. Let's now look at an example of how this can be done.

EXAMPLE

Read this passage from Emily Brontë's classic novel, *Wuthering Heights*. The book tells the story of two families — the Earnshaws and the Lintons — and centres round the dark and passionate character of Heathcliff, an orphan brought home by Mr Earnshaw who grows up and falls in love with his daughter, Catherine. She, however, marries the more refined Edgar Linton and Heathcliff vows revenge on both the Earnshaw and Linton families.

This extract comes from Chapter Six when the main participants are still in their childhood. Young Heathcliff and Catherine slip away from the Earnshaw home (Wuthering Heights) and peer through the windows of the Linton home (Thrushcross Grange) and witness a very different lifestyle from the one they are used to.

We ran from the top of the Heights to the park, without stopping — Catherine completely beaten in the race; because she was barefoot. You'll have to seek for her shoes in the bog tomorrow. We crept through a broken hedge, groped our way up the path, and planted ourselves on a flower-plot under the drawing-room window. The light came from thence; they had not put up the shutters, and the curtains were only half closed. Both of us were able to look in by standing on the basement, and clinging to the ledge, and we saw — ah! it was beautiful — a splendid place carpeted with crimson, and crimson-covered chairs and tables, and a pure white ceiling bordered by gold, a shower of glass-drops hanging in silver chains from the centre and shimmering with little soft tapers. Old Mr. and Mrs. Linton were not there; Edgar and his sister had it entirely to themselves. Shouldn't they have been happy? We should have thought ourselves in heaven! And now, guess what your good children were doing? Isabella — I believe she is eleven, a year younger than Cathy — lay screaming at the farther end of the room, shrieking as if witches were running red-hot needles into her. Edgar stood on the hearth weeping silently, and in the middle of the table sat a little dog, shaking its paw and yelping; which, from their mutual accusations, we understood they had nearly pulled in two between them. The idiots! That was their pleasure! to quarrel who should hold a heap of warm hair, and each begin to cry because both, after struggling to get it, refused to take it. We laughed outright at the petted things; we did despise them! When would you catch me wishing to have what Catherine wanted? or find us by ourselves, seeking entertainment in yelling, and sobbing, and rolling on the ground, divided by the whole room? I'd not exchange, for a thousand lives, my condition here, for Edgar Linton's at Thrushcross Grange.

A student has decided to write a review on the theme of the connections between setting and character in *Wuthering Heights*. In the course of her essay, she looks at the above extract in some depth. This part of her essay is reproduced below and should give you an idea of the kind of commentary to be found in a good review.

One section of the novel where the description of the setting helped me to understand the characters better was the scene where Catherine and Heathcliff look though the window of Thrushcross Grange and see Edgar Linton and his sister Isabella for the first time. I felt that in some respects the window was being used symbolically here: the physical barrier separating the two pairs of children represented the gulf between them caused by the differences in the way they had been brought up. Even the fact that Heathcliff and Catherine were "standing on the basement and clinging to the ledge" indicates their social position as outsiders. There is a clear contrast between Catherine and Heathcliff who are used to the rugged outdoors and the Lintons who have led a life of pampered indoor luxury. This came through in the author's word choice. The references to "a broken hedge", the manner in which the children "groped" up the path and Cathy's loss of her shoes in the mud contrast strongly with the delicacy and splendour of the interior of the Lintons' house with its "pure white ceiling bordered by gold . . . shimmering with little soft tapers". I thought it was particularly significant that instead of simply using the noun "chandelier" Heathcliff used a long roundabout description — "a shower of glass-drops hanging in silver chains from the centre, and shimmering with little soft tapers" — indicating that the way of life he was describing was so unfamiliar to him that he did not even know the correct name for this object.

✔   This paragraph deals with a specific point as indicated in the opening topic sentence. It sticks to this point and does not move into general discussion. The student reveals her detailed knowledge of the text. In other words, understanding of the text is shown.

✔   Evidence and quotations are provided to back up the points — in other words, there is analysis of the text.

✔   The writer uses a personal tone and explains why she found the aspects quoted were effective — in other words, there is some evaluation of the text.

✔   There is an awareness of literary terms such as symbolism and a line of thought is developed. Spelling, grammar, etc., are correct. In other words, the expression is sound.

Appendix: *Recommended Texts for the Personal Study*

There are thousands of texts of literary merit which would make suitable choices. The following list contains only a small selection of these. Generally, most works by the authors listed would prove suitable, but remember to check with a teacher or tutor. (The division into sections is for convenience: some books could fall into several categories. Because of the wide range available, only a few works of non-fiction are included; these are marked with an asterisk *.)

PRE TWENTIETH CENTURY AUTHORS

Jane Austen: e.g., *Persuasion*. Anne Elliot regrets being "persuaded" by a well-meaning friend to abandon a relationship with a young naval officer. Later, she learns to make her own judgments. Very strong on characterisation, Austen's novels include acute observation of morals, manners and social foibles. The vain, the mercenary and the self-indulgent are strongly condemned.

The Brontë sisters (Charlotte, Anne and Emily) wrote powerful novels which often consider the status of women in 19th century society. There is much scope for discussion of characters and themes, but settings are also memorable. Most famous is Emily's *Wuthering Heights*, describing the passionate love affair between Catherine Earnshaw and Heathcliff which has repercussions in the next generation also. Charlotte's *Jane Eyre* describes the struggle of an orphan girl to survive in a world where she is at first unloved and rejected.

Joseph Conrad: Conrad's stories are mainly of the sea or exploration. They are strong on character and atmosphere and depict themes such as endurance. *The Shadow Line* is a short novel about a captain's delight at receiving his first command of a sailing ship. However, it becomes becalmed and there is an epidemic on board.

Charles Dickens: e.g., *Great Expectations*. Pip, the hero, learns to appreciate real values after an experiment in social climbing. Dickens is a writer noted for his masterly characterisation, use of settings and social observation, together with a witty style. The longer novels are very complex and demanding, however.

George Eliot: e.g., *Silas Marner*. Silas, a miser, is devastated when he is robbed of his gold, but he finds consolation when he takes on the guardianship of a lost child. Eliot's writings are admired for their complex character development and perceptive moral observations.

Thomas Hardy: Hardy's novels are set in Dorset. They have vivid settings and descriptions and consider the interplay of character and fate in shaping an individual's life. In *Far from the Madding Crowd*, the vain Bathsheba Everdene juggles relationships with three men, ending up humbler and wiser. Other possible choices include *The Return of the Native*, *Tess of the D'Urbervilles*, *The Woodlanders* and *Jude the Obscure*.

Henry James: e.g., *The Aspern Papers*, an atmospheric novella set in Venice about an unscrupulous collector of literary memorabilia who is sure he can manipulate two elderly ladies into giving him what he wants. Do not be deterred by James's "difficult" reputation: the shorter novels, such as *Washington Square*, *Daisy Miller* or *The Turn of the Screw*, are particularly suitable.

Ivan Turgenev: One of Russia's foremost novelists, Turgenev is less difficult than might be expected. *First Love* is a novella about a boy who falls in love for the first time, only to discover that his own father is his rival.

H.G. Wells: e.g., *The War of the Worlds*, in which the Martians invade Earth. Pioneering writing in science fiction.

SCOTTISH AUTHORS

Iain Banks: Also a writer of science fiction under the name Iain M. Banks, this author is constantly inventive and very appealing to young readers. In *Espedair Street*, a former rock star attempts to return to normality after the wild excesses of his touring days.

Elspeth Barker: *O Caledonia*. A study of a sixteen-year-old girl growing up in an eccentric family. Vivid black comedy.

George Douglas Brown: *The House with the Green Shutters*. Bleak story of the downfall of the wealthy, ambitious John Gourlay and the disintegration of his family.

George Mackay Brown: e.g., *Greenvoe*. The culture of a rural Orkney community is threatened by "Black Star", a sinister top secret uranium enterprise. Very vivid in his portrayal of setting and characters, this Orcadian author's poetry and short stories are also highly recommended.

John Buchan: An early twentieth century writer of thrillers, e.g., *The Thirty-Nine Steps*. Hero Richard Hannay outwits a group of German spies before the outbreak of World War One. Strong on settings and suspense.

Iain Crichton-Smith: e.g., *Consider the Lilies*. Set at the time of the Highland Clearances, Mrs Scott is one of the victims of this cruel policy. The author's poetry and short stories are also highly recommended.

David Daiches: e.g., * *Two Worlds*. Autobiography describing his childhood in Edinburgh and the dual cultures, Jewish and Scottish, which he reconciled so successfully.

George Friel: e.g., *Mr Alfred M.A*. A middle-aged schoolteacher becomes infatuated with one of his pupils. Lucid style and sympathetic character portrayal.

Janice Galloway: e.g., *The Trick is To Keep Breathing*. The story of a woman battling mental illness and failed relationships, this is nevertheless wryly humorous.

Edward Gaitens: *Dance of the Apprentices*. The novel follows the fortunes of a group of young men living in the Gorbals in the early part of the century, and describes their attempts to break free of the limitations of their background. Slightly dated, but interesting for its social documentation.

Lewis Grassic Gibbon: *Sunset Song*. The first of a trilogy, this charts the decay of an isolated rural community in north east Scotland around the time of the first world war, and centres on the life of a talented girl, Chris Guthrie. Strong characterisation and poetic style. Grassic Gibbon's short stories are also recommended.

Robin Jenkins: e.g., *The Changeling*. A well meaning but misguided Glasgow school-teacher tries to improve the lot of a pupil from a deprived background. Vivid and moving character portrayal.

James Kennaway: *Tunes of Glory*. A new colonel arrives to take charge of a battalion. The resulting clash of personalities with the "acting" colonel creates bitter divisions within the group.

A.L. Kennedy: A young, contemporary author. e.g., *Looking for the Possible Dance*, the story of Margaret who works in a community centre, and her relationships with three men, her father, her boyfriend and her employer, who are all dependent on her in different ways.

Liz Lochhead: e.g., *Perfect Days*. A play about a successful top-class hairdresser coming to terms with the fact that she is getting older and her personal life is empty. Very witty writer of drama and poetry with mainly Glasgow settings.

A. McArthur and **H. Kingsley Long:** *No Mean City.* The story of the rise and fall of a razor-wielding gang leader in Glasgow's Gorbals in the 1920s, this novel also vividly depicts living conditions in the slums at that period.

Guy McCrone: *Wax Fruit.* A trilogy following the fortunes of members of a prosperous Glasgow family in the late nineteenth century. Strong on social detail.

William McIlvanney: e.g., *Docherty.* The story of a miner and the conflict he encounters through his religion and his relationships with his sons.

Tony Roper: *The Steamie:* A play set in one of Glasgow's public wash-houses which reveals through comedy the character and courage of the women who gather there.

Robert Louis Stevenson: Many of his novels, such as *Dr Jekyll and Mr Hyde* or *Weir of Hermiston,* explore the theme of good and evil in human nature. Settings are very important. His short stories such as *Markheim* often contain a supernatural element.

20TH CENTURY "CLASSICS" (Written mainly in the earlier years of the century)

(i)   *War and Adventure*

H.E. Bates: e.g., *Fair Stood the Wind for France.* A British airman is shot down in France. He has to have his arm amputated, and is dependent on the good will of the French civilians who risk their lives by helping him.

William Golding: e.g., *Lord of the Flies.* Describing a group of young boys stranded on an island without adult supervision, the story deals with the perennial theme of good and evil. Clear-eyed, although pessimistic, observation of the human condition.

Graham Greene: e.g., *Our Man in Havana:* a vacuum cleaner salesman pretends to be a spy, but matters become serious when his inventions are taken seriously. Greene is a stylish writer, particularly good at creating the murky world of espionage and intrigue.

Joseph Heller: *Catch Twenty-Two.* A black and surreal comedy describing the lives of American pilots in World War II.

Ernest Hemingway: e.g., *For Whom the Bell Tolls.* Robert Jordan, an American fighting the fascists in the Spanish Civil War, is ordered to dynamite a bridge. During the few days he spends in the mountains with a small guerrilla band he learns the moral issues are much more complex than he had realised.

Erich Maria Remarque: e.g., *All Quiet on the Western Front.* This novel describes the harrowing experiences of a young German private in the first world war who realises all too clearly that the Germans are losing.

John Steinbeck: e.g., *The Moon is Down.* When a large nation invades a small one, they discover that the inhabitants are not so easy to subdue as they had anticipated.

(ii) *Effects of society on individuals and relationships*

Albert Camus: *The Outsider.* The story of Mersault who refuses to conform to the expectations society has of him and ends up facing the guillotine because of his refusal to compromise.

Scott Fitzgerald: e.g., *The Great Gatsby.* Jay Gatsby, whose origins are humble, is obsessed with the beautiful but shallow Daisy, a girl from a wealthy upper-class background. The novel observes his doomed attempt to enter her exclusive world.

Aldous Huxley: e.g., *Brave New World.* A chilling account of a future world which attempts to eliminate all human problems by means of technology or more subtle mind-bending.

Harper Lee: *To Kill a Mocking-Bird.* A little girl is forced to confront the evils of racism in 1930s Alabama when her lawyer father is asked to defend a negro on a charge of raping a white woman.

George Orwell: e.g., *Nineteen Eighty-Four.* The story of a forbidden love affair in a world where every thought is policed and "Big Brother" is always watching you.

Alexander Solzhenitsyn: e.g., *A Day in the Life of Ivan Denisovitch.* The story of the hardships suffered by an internee in a bleak Soviet labour camp and his constant struggle for survival with dignity.

Edith Wharton: e.g., *The House of Mirth.* Lily longs for the good things in life, but she cannot quite bring herself to abandon the man she loves in favour of a more financially favourable marriage. Excellent social observation of New England society where wealth is everything.

(iii) *Novels centred around interesting or unusual individual characters*

Truman Capote: *Breakfast at Tiffany's.* The story of Holly Golightly, a beautiful New York socialite who has completely re-invented herself and remains an innocent despite her sleazy surroundings.

E.M. Forster: e.g., *A Room with a View.* Set largely in Venice. The heroine Lucy learns to make her own judgments on character and to resist the snobbishness of those around her.

Daphne du Maurier: *Rebecca* tells the story of a new young wife obsessed and intimidated by thoughts of her beautiful dead predecessor. The character of Mrs Danvers, the sinister housekeeper, is a particularly memorable creation.

L.P. Hartley: e.g., *The Go-Between.* Leo is invited to spend the holidays with his wealthy friend Marcus, but problems arise with Marcus's beautiful sister Marian when she employs him as the "go-between" in her secret love affair.

D.H. Lawrence: e.g., *The Virgin and the Gypsy.* Yvette, the daughter of a vicar, becomes fascinated by a gypsy after having her fortune told. Lawrence, as ever, sides with those who rebel against conventional morality.

J.D. Salinger: e.g., *The Catcher in the Rye.* Holden Caulfield is a confused teenager who cannot come to terms with the adult world and its "phoneyness". After being expelled from school, Holden returns home, but he does not know where his life is going.

Jack Schaefer: e.g., *Shane*. Shane is the mysterious gunman who comes to the rescue of the homesteaders whose livelihood is being threatened by the more powerful ranch owners. The story is narrated by the young son of one of the homesteaders.

Evelyn Waugh: e.g., *Brideshead Revisited*. During the war, Charles Ryder "revisits" a stately home, Brideshead. The novel then tells in flashback of his former relationship with the family, in particular with the son, Sebastian and the daughter, Julia.

CONTEMPORARY WRITERS

(i) *War and Adventure*

J.G. Ballard: e.g., *Empire of the Sun*. Based on the writer's own experiences, the novel tells of twelve-year-old Jim's experiences in the second world war amid the horrors of a Japanese concentration camp in Shanghai.

Louis de Bernières: e.g., *Captain Corelli's Mandolin*. Captain Corelli is an Italian, part of the occupying force on the Greek island of Cephalonia. There he falls in love with a Greek girl.

Thomas Eidson: *St Agnes Stand*. A superior western in which a gunman on the run is faced with the choice of saving himself or stopping to protect a group of nuns and children who are being threatened by Red Indians who have already tortured and murdered one of their number.

Sebastian Faulks: e.g., *Birdsong*, a novel set in France which tells the story of a young Englishman just before and during the first world war. A question of identity two generations later provides an interesting twist.

Charles Frazier: e.g., *Cold Mountain*. A soldier wounded in the American Civil War makes a long and arduous journey home to the woman he loves.

Brian Keenan: *An Evil Cradling*. The true story of the author's experiences as a hostage in Beirut.

Thomas Keneally: e.g., *Schindler's Ark*. Oskar Schindler is a self-indulgent bon viveur, a friend of prominent Nazis, but nevertheless becomes a saviour to his Jewish workers.

Joe Simpson: e.g., *Touching the Void*. The harrowing true story of how his mountaineering companion cut the connecting rope after Simpson fell and left him for dead, and how Simpson struggled back to safety.

(ii) *Effects of society on individuals and relationships*

Pat Barker: e.g., *Regeneration*. Set at Edinburgh's Craiglockhart hospital for shell-shock victims, the novel mainly focuses on a psychiatrist, Dr Rivers, and one of his patients, Billy Prior. This novel is the first part of a trilogy.

Suzanne Berne: *A Crime in the Neighbourhood*. A psychological novel rather than a mere who-dun-it, the book describes the repercussions in a quiet residential suburb of Washington DC after a young boy is murdered.

Ruth Prawer Jhabvala: e.g., *Heat and Dust*. A girl goes to India hoping to learn something about her grandmother's life there. There she herself embarks on a love affair which has echoes of the tragic earlier one.

Frank McCourt: **Angela's Ashes*. The story of a desperately poor family living in Limerick. Frank's father is a feckless alcoholic and eventually deserts the family after which an even greater burden falls on his mother, Angela.

Bernard MacLaverty: e.g., *Cal*. Cal is a young Catholic who has been an unwilling accessory to an IRA murder. Later he meets and falls in love with the victim's wife. McLaverty's short stories are also highly recommended.

Brian Moore: e.g., *Lies of Silence*. The wife of a hotel manager in Northern Ireland is taken hostage. Her safety is only guaranteed if he will place a bomb in his hotel. The manager's moral dilemma is increased as he is estranged from his wife and is having an affair with another woman.

Arundhati Roy: *The God of Small Things*. A novel describing a wealthy Indian family and the tragic repercussions of a love affair between one of its members and a man of the caste of "untouchables".

William Trevor: e.g., *Two Lives*, a pair of novellas, including *My House in Umbria*. A romantic novelist who has settled in Italy is on a train when a terrorist bomb explodes, killing most of those in her carriage. She generously offers the use of her home to the survivors for their convalescence when they come out of hospital. She becomes involved with their lives, and gradually the truth about the terrorist emerges.

(iii) *Novels centred around interesting or unusual characters*

Kate Atkinson: e.g., *Human Croquet*. Sixteen-year-old Isobel wonders constantly what happened to her glamorous mother Eliza who left suddenly when she was a little girl. As the murky truth surrounding Eliza's disappearance begins to emerge, Isobel finds her grip on reality loosening.

Margaret Atwood: e.g., *Alias Grace*. Set in the nineteenth century, this tells the story of mild-mannered Grace, an expert in quilt-making, in prison for life for having allegedly brutally murdered her employer.

Beryl Bainbridge: e.g., *The Dressmaker*. Set in the second world war, naïve Rita is dazzled when she meets Ira, an American G.I. Rita's protective aunt, the "dressmaker", takes matters into her own hands when Ira proves unfaithful.

Roddy Doyle: e.g., *Paddy Clark, Ha Ha Ha*. The highly comic yet unsentimental account of the life of a young boy living in Northern Ireland who has to come to terms with the break-up of his parents' marriage.

Margaret Drabble: e.g., *The Millstone*. Written in the sixties, but still topical, this novel looks at the changing feelings of a teenage unmarried mother towards her baby.

John Fowles: e.g., *The Collector*. The story of an obsession: a gauche young man wins a huge sum of money and is then emboldened to kidnap and imprison a beautiful art student he has fantasised about.

Susan Hill: e.g., *The Woman in Black*. A Victorian style ghost story. Whenever a mysterious woman appears, a child's death inevitably follows. A young lawyer becomes involved in the mystery when he acts as the executor to the late occupant of Eelmarsh House, a location with a gruesome history.

Ishiguro Kurosawa: *The Remains of the Day*. An unusual story of a repressed butler who has misplaced priorities where love and duty are concerned.

Jennifer Johnston: e.g., *The Old Jest*. Eighteen-year-old Nancy has never known her father. A meeting with a mysterious man at the beach triggers her imagination, but she becomes unwittingly involved in the dark world of the IRA.

DRAMATISTS

Alan Ayckbourn: Ayckbourn looks perceptively and often humorously at the relationships of ordinary people, e.g., *Joking Apart*, a play in which a generous and apparently popular family gradually become aware of the resentment and envy of their friends and neighbours.

Henrik Ibsen: e.g., *An Enemy of the People*. The brilliant but naïve Dr Stockmann becomes an outcast when he wants to reveal the truth about the pollution of the town's new baths which are promising to bring wealth to his community. Typically, Ibsen's plays open with an apparently serene and happy scene. Layers of hypocrisy are then stripped away to reveal ugly truths.

Arthur Miller: e.g., *All My Sons*. A play about a son being confronted with some very unsavoury truths about the past life of the father he worships. Miller was strongly influenced by Ibsen. In his plays, ordinary people attain tragic status.

Terence Rattigan: e.g., *The Winslow Boy*. Arthur Winslow takes on the British Establishment to prove his son's innocence when he is expelled from school accused of stealing. However, his courageous moral stand imposes enormous financial and emotional burdens on his family and himself.

William Shakespeare: Any play. Quite a difficult, but virtually always a rewarding choice.

Bernard Shaw: e.g., *Pygmalion*. Speech expert Professor Higgins places a bet with his friend Colonel Pickering that he can pass off Cockney flower-seller Eliza Doolittle as a "lady". The play's themes include social and sexual equality, two of the many social reforms Shaw supported.

R.C. Sherriff: *Journey's End*. A first world war play describing a few days in the life of a British company in the front line in 1918. Although the language is dated, the plight of the officers remains vivid, particularly that of twenty-one-year-old Stanhope who has to cope with both a dependence on alcohol and an unwelcome arrival from home.

Oscar Wilde: Wilde's frothy dialogue overlies serious comment on the manners and morals of society. *The Importance of Being Ernest* is a brilliant comedy which eventually unearths the truth about the hero's identity after he had famously been found as a baby in "a handbag" at Victoria Station.

Tennessee Williams: e.g., *The Glass Menagerie*. Shy, crippled Laura is subjected to her mother's very embarrassing attempts at match-making with one of her brother's colleagues who turns out to be an old schoolmate. Williams's plays are very personal: Laura's character is based on his own handicapped sister.

ACKNOWLEDGEMENTS

We are extremely grateful to the following for permission to use copyright material in this book.

Extract from *THE GO-BETWEEN*
by L.P. Hartley.
First published Hamish Hamilton 1953.
© 1953 by L.P. Hartley.
This edition copyright © Douglas Brooks-Davies 1997.
Reproduced by permission of Penguin Books Ltd.

The Bike
by Fred Urquhart.
Reprinted by permission of Dr. Colin Affleck literary executor
and The Estate of Fred Urquhart.

Extract from *The Girl at the Lion D'Or*
by Sebastian Faulks
Reprinted by permission of Vintage Publishers.

It's a sore point but if there's no pain, there's no gain
by Ian Wood.
Reprinted by permission of The Scotsman Publications Ltd.

Extract from
Get ready to throw out your TV set.
The next generation just isn't interested anymore
by Gareth McLean
Reprinted by permission of The Scotsman Publications Ltd.

Extract from *Consider the Lilies*
by Iain Crichton Smith.
Published as a Canongate Classic in 1987
by Canongate Books, 14 High Street, Edinburgh, EH1 1TE
and reprinted in 1998.

Orders: please contact Bookpoint Ltd, 130 Milton Park, Abingdon, Oxon OX14 4SB. Telephone: (44) 01235 827720. Fax: (44) 01235 400454. Lines are open from 9.00–5.00, Monday to Saturday, with a 24 hour message answering service. You can also order through our website www.hoddereducation.co.uk.

Papers used in this book are natural, renewable and recyclable products. They are made from wood grown in sustainable forests. The logging and manufacturing processes conform to the environmental regulations of the country of origin.

British Library Cataloguing in Publication Data
A catalogue record for this title is available from the British Library

ISBN: 978-0-71698020-9

Published by Hodder Gibson, 2a Christie Street, Paisley PA1 1NB.
Tel: 0141 848 1609; Fax: 0141 889 6315; Email: hoddergibson@hodder.co.uk
First Published 2000; Revised Edition Published 2002
Impression number   12 11 10 9 8 7 6 5
Year   2010 2009 2008

Copyright © 2000, 2002 Mary M Firth and Andrew G Ralston

Printed in Great Britain for Hodder Gibson, 2a Christie Street, Paisley, PA1 1NB, Scotland, UK by Martins the Printers.